MW00574383

THE AUTOMATIC MARKETING MACHINE

THE AUTOMATIC MARKETING MACHINE

RJON ROBINS & DANNY DECKER

ForbesBooks

Published by ForbesBooks, Charleston, South Carolina.
Member of Advantage Media Group.

ForbesBooks is a registered trademark, and the ForbesBooks colophon is a trademark of Forbes Media, LLC.

Printed in the United States of America.

10 9 8 7 6 5 4 3 2 1

ISBN: 978-1-95588-414-3
LCCN: 2022905023

Cover design by Matthew Morse.
Layout design by Wesley Strickland.

This custom publication is intended to provide accurate information and the opinions of the author in regard to the subject matter covered. It is sold with the understanding that the publisher, Advantage|ForbesBooks, is not engaged in rendering legal, financial, or professional services of any kind. If legal advice or other expert assistance is required, the reader is advised to seek the services of a competent professional.

 Advantage Media Group is proud to be a part of the Tree Neutral® program. Tree Neutral offsets the number of trees consumed in the production and printing of this book by taking proactive steps such as planting trees in direct proportion to the number of trees used to print books. To learn more about Tree Neutral, please visit www.treeneutral.com.

Since 1917, Forbes has remained steadfast in its mission to serve as the defining voice of entrepreneurial capitalism. ForbesBooks, launched in 2016 through a partnership with Advantage Media Group, furthers that aim by helping business and thought leaders bring their stories, passion, and knowledge to the forefront in custom books. Opinions expressed by ForbesBooks authors are their own. To be considered for publication, please visit www.forbesbooks.com.

CONTENTS

INTRODUCTION

Y ou have finally found it. A very special place created for small business owners who are seeking to answer that common, nagging question: "Our products and services are the best around, so why am I always scrambling desperately to find new customers and clients?"

All businesses face the same challenge: how to attract a steady stream of the right kinds of customers predictably, reliably, and consistently in order to produce steady (and growing) cash flow, to create enough confidence that you don't have to accept work from crazy clients and customers just to make payroll next week!

If this doesn't resonate with you, chances are you're not the owner of the business you work for. If you do own a business, then it probably does. And regardless of what industry you're in, no matter how big or small your team may be and irrespective of past success, then we want to congratulate you for being an entrepreneur.

You are the engine of the world.

Rest assured: while you hold this book in your hands, you are with other like-minded entrepreneurs—friends who know what it's like to sit in the seat where the buck actually stops.

This book is 100 percent based upon real-world, direct response, education-based marketing strategies that have the power to consistently, predictably attract the right kinds of customers and clients to your business. Each strategy you're soon to discover in the pages that follow has been proven by thousands of small business owners in every industry you can imagine, operating in large cities and small towns and everything in between. You're going to meet many of them in this book. They're men and women of all ages, all attitudes, all walks of life; some of them are right handed, some left. Anyone can do this!

You have worked hard, created a solid reputation, and done great work with a long list of happy and appreciative customers. But you've discovered that just doing great work doesn't automatically attract prospective new customers.

Let's get this out of the way right now: the business owners who are out there bragging that they get all their business by reputation and referral ... either they're lying to you or their business isn't serving nearly as many clients and customers as it could be (a polite way to say they're broke). Or else they are naive to the facts, and there is a grown-up attending to the marketing of their business so that the children at the kiddies' table don't have to concern themselves with where the food comes from.

So you've tried marketing. You've spent serious money on ads that didn't work, direct mail that underdelivered, pay-per-click advertising that drained your bank account dry, and probably a host of other approaches, none of which delivered the results promised or expected.

Like most entrepreneurs, you sometimes feel confused and overwhelmed. You're getting hammered on all sides with "consultants" telling you to do one thing or another and feeling like you have to press harder to do more and more—just to get by each month.

We are here to help you—to mute all that noise and provide you with a set of practical and proven principles, not just theories, tactics, or the latest technology. We'll also be sharing the resources you'll need to consistently, automatically attract customers who are ready, willing, and able to engage your business. And by that we mean a scalable marketing machine—not only to attract new leads but also to convert leads into appointments, appointments into customers, and multiply one customer into two, four, and eight.

FREE BONUS MATERIALS

We've created a marketing toolbox packed with tools, spreadsheets, templates, case studies, bonus lessons, and step-by-step instructional guides to help you as you learn and implement the teachings in this book. They're all available to you, as a reader of this book, for instant download, complimentary. We strongly suggest that you download the toolbox now so you have these materials available as you begin to read.

Scan the QR code below for instant access:

Marketing is an ever-changing world, as new media seems to pop up every day. But if you learn the principles that allow some of the most successful businesses in the country to attract a steady stream of new prospects, you can make any media work, in any market, at any time, regardless of what might be happening with everyone else.

When you develop a machine that automatically feeds new prospects and customers to your business on a daily basis, you will never again have to feel the anxiety of wondering when or where your next infusion of cash flow will come from! In fact, you will finally know the answer to the question that haunts so many hundreds of thousands of struggling entrepreneurs:

"Our products and services are some of the best around, so why am I always scrambling desperately to find new customers and clients?"

Where Did These Ideas Originate?

These ideas began with a discovery—or, more accurately, a series of discoveries—that could well form the most important realization you'll ever arrive at as an entrepreneur.

Because it's not enough to deliver a great product or service. You also have to understand how to market so you can have customers to deliver products and services to. In other words, you have to understand marketing. You can't just expect to do great work and therefore have that fact automatically attract customers to you. It just doesn't work like that in the real world.

Let's think about this rationally for a minute—and you'll understand just how misguided most business owners are when they brag about relying on referrals for all their business.

Whether you've recognized it or not, you are mostly in the business of solving other people's problems. The first thing your customers and clients probably want to do as soon as you've solved their problem is put that problem behind them and not think about it anymore. So it's not like most of them are going around looking for opportunities to tell other people about your services. (At least not until we engineer a way for that to happen!)

Which means that it's naive to believe that customers evangelizing for your business is going to figure into the top ten, or even top one hundred, things any one of your customers is going to be thinking about on a daily basis. This is why when entrepreneurs go around bragging that they settle for only having as much business as referrals may bring, they are either lying, and in fact they're out doing a lot of marketing that they're just not telling you about, or they're starving for business.

If they're starving for business—which is a condition affecting a statistically high percentage of small business owners—it could be they're telling you the truth about passively waiting for the phone to ring, thereby leaving a mountain of opportunity for other entrepreneurs (like you), or they could be engaged in the wrong kind of marketing.

Either way, we believe that business owners who neglect the marketing of their businesses neglect their responsibility to actively market the availability of valuable products and services that give their customers the opportunity to have better lives!

Of course, most of the owners of struggling businesses who settle for just waiting around for the phone to ring, or who rely on the crap that passes for marketing for most small businesses, have likely never learned about the sort of direct response, trackable, education-based, highly ethical, and wildly profitable upstream marketing you'll be exposed to in this book. So maybe we can give them a break. But the fact that *you* are reading these words right now means you are likely more entrepreneurially mature than most small business owners. And while those business owners still hold on to fairy tales about how "being the best leads to success," you already know that

- you can be the most skilled technician in the world and still starve with no customers;

- you may offer the very best services in your market and still starve with no new customers;

- you can have a positive attitude that Norman Vincent Peale would envy and be as motivated as a participant at a Tony Robbins seminar and still starve with no new customers;

- you can stand willing to provide great value, great service, great expertise and still starve with no new customers;

- your business can literally be a paragon of virtue, with the world seemingly singing your praises 24-7, and even as you bask in their applause, you can still starve!

The realization you've probably come to, which led you to this book, is this: you could very well starve, you won't get rich, and you certainly won't have peace of mind ... unless and until you have an affordable, efficient, dependable means of attracting a sufficient flow of qualified prospects, customers, and clients.

Most business owners sort of know this, but they still focus on everything *but* the one thing that will make all the difference in the world to their success: ***marketing***.

Entrepreneurs have a responsibility to market their services. People really need your products and services! But despite all the advertisements everywhere you look, it's actually pretty hard for most people to find the help that they need.

Need proof?

Consider the fact that even a simple search on the internet produces so many advertisements. Of course, it's possible that all those businesses spending all that money for all those ads are just complete and total idiots who don't bother to track or measure return on investment (ROI), and so they don't know they're throwing their money away. And certainly, that's exactly the case for many of them. But isn't it more likely that the only reason you see so many businesses advertising so much on the internet (and elsewhere) is because, even if it could work a lot better, it must be producing at least some business for them?

In other words, the fact that so many people find themselves with *no better choice than to conduct a Google search* to find the help they're looking for is strong evidence that there are a lot of people out there who need help and don't know where to find it.

Marketing allows business owners who seriously study and embrace it to live up to the moral obligation all entrepreneurs should take seriously: to ensure that when a prospective new customer needs their services, they already know how to find them!

Marketing also addresses the responsibilities all business owners have to all those who are depending on the business to remain viable—by generating a steady stream of prospective new prospects, which

Your Automatic Marketing Machine will become one of the most valuable assets of your business.

translates to predictable and growing cash flow for the business.

When built, tested, refined, and proven to work—day in, day out—even when you're not there working, your Automatic Marketing Machine will become one of the most valuable assets of your business.

In addition, it is critical to understand that many of the frustrations and internal problems you're likely experiencing with your business today are because you *don't* have a good marketing machine in place. Many businesses stand ready to provide great products and services delivered by caring employees with noble motivations. But they fail because they don't have enough sales opportunities. To paraphrase Thoreau, most entrepreneurs lead lives of quiet desperation because they don't know how to create a steady and sufficient supply of new prospects, customers, and clients for their business.

Why This Book? Why Now?

I—RJon—first met my coauthor Danny when he and his business partner snuck into an event that I was hosting for a few hundred of the entrepreneurs whose small businesses my own firm helps to manage.

Danny crashed our gate with a style that caught my attention and eventually earned my respect. Good thing Danny handled himself the way that he did, and good thing I kept an open mind, because that first encounter could have gone either way, and I am so very glad it went the right way. It was 2012. I was forty-one years old. Danny was just twenty-six years old. In the years that followed, Danny has been a client of mine, and I've been a client of his. We've had the opportunity to collaborate on a number of projects for each other's businesses and for mutual clients of ours. The common thread in our work together: a mutual obsession with the philosophy of direct response marketing and the power direct response marketing has to transform any business in any industry when properly applied and harnessed.

The *principles* in this book have been taught in various forms for hundreds of years and have been tested over and again by businesses of all shapes, sizes, industries, and locations that use them to create a steady flow of new clients and customers. Throughout this book you'll discover how entrepreneurs just like you have used the very same strategies to scale, grow, and differentiate their businesses—to rise above the competition and to quickly demand (and receive) top dollar for their products and services.

We're here to give you the entire vision plus the architecture that will allow you to make this vision a reality. To help you become the prosperous owner of a *real* business and to free you from the endless, desperate need for the next new customers and clients.

The teaching in this book will allow you to create certainty and security and stability. It will give you the blueprint to create a continuous and steady inflow of desired customers and clients who trust your business, rely on your business, and refer their friends, family, and/or business acquaintances to your business. The teaching in this book will allow you to create equity and wealth, not just day-to-day income—though it will help with that too.

This does *not* require any special background—just the commitment to use what you discover. You can apply it to any kind of practice serving any kind of market; in fact you'll soon meet entrepreneurs in this book who will demonstrate exactly how this *system* worked for them.

For now, know that *you can* build an Automatic Marketing Machine—and transform your business forever—with what you'll discover in the following pages.

Let's begin.

CHAPTER ONE

LET'S CUT THE BS AND MAKE YOUR SMALL BUSINESS MORE PROFITABLE

"The truth will set you free. But first it will piss you off!"
—GLORIA STEINEM

The truth of the matter is that you have been lied to for a very long time. Or if it makes you feel any better, you've been fed a whole bunch of bullshit about how to market your business. And <u>that</u> is why you are where you are with your business instead of where we know you want to be.

Where you may find yourself is frustrated, scared, intimidated, insecure, and overwhelmed. Yes, it can be very frustrating to know in your heart that you have the capacity to do great work, if only you could find better clients and customers that would give you the opportunity to show the world what you're made of.

It can be very frustrating, too, when you find yourself in the office in the middle of the night or on the weekends instead of with your family, enjoying the fruits of your labors, and all because your business can't bring in enough customers to afford you the confidence (or the cash flow) to hire the help you need so that you can stay focused on only the highest and best use of your time, energies, and talents. It can be pretty scary, too, not knowing where the next customer is going to come from, especially toward the end of the month!

And it's even worse when you see other businesses with less experience and less expertise in your local market who seem to be getting plenty of customers to make the long-term, courageous business decisions you know you'd be able to make in terms of hiring, training, investing in equipment ... and turning down the wrong customers or even the right customers who have the wrong needs.

It can be *very* frustrating to see these business owners making the decisions you wish you could be making, doing the things with their businesses you wish you could do with yours, and living the life you imagined when you decided to start your business ... all because they seem to have figured something out that for some reason still eludes you.

Well, we have some good news and some bad news.

The bad news is that much of this book is probably going to piss you off.

The good news is that if you follow the very simple instructions you'll find throughout this book in plain English, detailing precisely how and why to build an Automatic Marketing Machine for your business, it will also set you free!

So let's get to it.

Who has lied to me, and why?

That's what you want to know, right? Well, at the risk of distracting you from taking action that will help you make things better, we'll indulge your curiosity for a bit. But only so you can get it out of your system so that we can devote the rest of this book to helping you recover from the damage already done.

Let's start by defining the terms:

First, let's talk about truth. Truth is reality; reality is truth. In other words, it is what it is, and one of the fundamental facts about truth is that while it can be changed by a person's *actions*, reality cannot be changed merely by your wishes or wants or desires and not even by how good a person you are. Truth is not in the eye of the beholder. There is no such thing as a perceived reality. There are perceptions of reality, of course, but it's still reality that's being perceived differently by different people depending on their tools of perception. If you want your business to be more profitable, you'll take this point seriously: truth is reality, and reality is truth, and businesses that operate from a place of truth tend to be much more profitable, especially in the long run.

Lies are an intentional misrepresentation of a person's best understanding of the truth.

Mistakes are the result of a person being wrong about their best understanding of the truth but doing his or her best to express it as honestly as that person can.

Bullshit is created when a person who has not bothered to investigate, think through, analyze, or ascertain the truth about something nonetheless makes representations about it. The key element of bullshit is that the representations made could turn out to be correct or incorrect, but at the time the representations are made, the person making them hasn't bothered to figure it out one way or the other. That's what makes it bullshit. When you ask a person why they did or didn't do something and they have no explanation and it's obvious they didn't think it through, then that smell you smell is probably bullshit in the air.

So let's talk about who has lied to you about marketing, and why:

College professors. If they told you that you don't need to concern yourself with marketing, that just being the best would be enough to bring your business a steady stream of profitable prospects, then they were feeding you bullshit or else they were mistaken.

Your first boss. If your first boss told you that you wouldn't have to worry about marketing, then your first boss was probably lying to you. Why? Maybe because your first boss didn't want you to think about marketing because he or she wanted you to focus on just doing your job or because your first boss didn't want you to feel empowered, since we all know that whoever controls the flow of prospects to a business ultimately has the power to dictate terms to that business, and so maybe your first boss didn't want you to know that fact of life. Gee, I wonder why!

Your marketing vendors. Unless your marketing vendors have been asking you some very detailed questions about your financial goals, the value of your average sale, your sales conversion rates, your cost of goods sold, and your company's current and planned capacity to handle how much more business ... and unless your marketing vendors have been sitting with you every month to review campaign performance, metrics, A/B testing results, and ROI, then they're lying to you at least by omission. And if they've been feeding you a bunch of bullshit vanity metrics that don't matter or telling you that they can't or you shouldn't track response rates and ROI for every dollar you spend on marketing, well then, they've been actively lying to you. Or if your marketing vendor or whoever is managing the marketing in your business is a friend of yours and it makes you feel bad to admit that your friendly marketing vendor has been lying to you, well then, let's just say they're incompetent and don't know any better.

Whatever helps you sleep at night.

We're going to talk a *lot* about marketing vendors in this book—and most of what we're going to tell you isn't good.

That's because, we're sorry to say, most marketing vendors are flat-out terrible. Over the years, we've both seen horror story after horror story in which an unethical and/or incompetent marketing vendor collects fat retainer checks from an unsuspecting business owner—for months or even for years—and leaves them with nothing to show for their investment. It happens all the time. It's sad but true.

On the other hand, some marketing vendors are really great! And it's important that you have quality marketing vendors on your team if you're serious about building a mature, profitable, sustainable Automatic Marketing Machine for your business.

So to help you hire your next marketing vendor with confidence, we've identified and organized a list of proven, skilled, results-oriented vendors who abide by the marketing principles taught in this book and are committed to honesty and transparency. To view a list of marketing vendors who have been vetted and certified by our team, scan the QR code below or visit www.AutomaticMarketingMachine.com/Vendors.

So yes … you've been lied to. Probably by many different people. And you've probably been fed a lot of bullshit along the way too. But let's put the past behind us now—because by the time you're done with this book, you'll not only know how to recover from the damage they caused you, but you'll know how to create a marketing machine that will create a tremendous amount of growth, wealth, and freedom in your life.

The Key Fact about Your Business That You Must Embrace

Without a sufficient and steady supply of potable water, nothing else about your life really matters, because within about three days, you're going to die.

Similarly, without a steady supply of customers and clients with whom your business can exchange valuable products and/or services for money, nothing else about your business really matters, because within a matter of months, your business will die too.

Being more educated or talented or skilled or willing than others has *zero* value if your business has no customers.

Neither your most impressive professional credentials, the high esteem of your peers, the quality of your work, nor any of your past professional accomplishments can change this fact of life.

Neither will your willingness to work long hours at the expense of your family, your deep commitment to your craft, or your high ethics and professional standards save your business from its fate if it can't attract a sufficient quantity of high-quality prospects willing to exchange payment for a solution to their problem.

Being more educated or talented or skilled or willing than others has *zero* value if your business has no customers.

Plus, it shortchanges all concerned when you show up as less than the best version of yourself after too many days of stress and too many sleepless nights worrying where the next prospect will come from … and all the obvious and predictable ill effects that follow. Many business owners harm themselves and others—including their customers—by denying this reality. They desperately want to believe that better is better: having better credentials, having gone to a better school, having more or better experience, having more integrity or a better work ethic, having paid their dues, investing in better technology and tools … even offering objectively superior products and services! *Better should be enough.* And lest we get into an argument about that—we totally agree! Better *should* be enough.

Perhaps in an idyllic and just world, that would be so.

But not in *this* world.

In this world you are not automatically awarded what you deserve or think you deserve. It's not a pure meritocracy. If that were the case, there'd probably be no rich criminals and no poor priests.

Successful business owners know money moves about for its own reasons, and neither need nor deservingness are magnets for it. Instead cash flow depends on powerful, well-crafted, measurable strategies—a tried and true system—that works across all kinds of media.

At this point you're either getting it or else (sadly) you may be like most struggling small business owners, who keep experiencing undesirable results but still refuse to consider the possibility that what they believed from college professors, employers, and mentors about running a successful business might have been just plain wrong.

Fortunately there's a better way to attract clients and customers to your business, and it's the philosophy that this book is built upon: direct response marketing.

Direct response marketing dates back many hundreds of years. It's not new. It just works. In fact the most effective digital marketing today and all the marketing you see taking place in the metaverse that actually works … it's all based on tried and true direct response marketing principles.

Direct response marketing is as proven as any of the natural laws because it is rooted in the laws of nature. Unlike laws made by human beings, the laws of nature are nonnegotiable, and you can't appeal them. While you can ignore them (and many do), you cannot ignore the consequences of ignoring natural law, though many try.

Too many struggling entrepreneurs attempt, at their peril, to negotiate the laws of nature upon which direct response marketing is based. But you cannot negotiate with the wind. You cannot appeal gravity. You cannot stop the tides. But if you have the courage, you will learn to harness these natural laws and let them work for you to carry you toward your goals.

A much more effective strategy than continuing to ignore, rationalize, justify, or argue about it when your business produces undesirable results, year after year, is to change your strategy.

Don't just defend the unprofitable actions already taken. Don't be an advocate for the forces that are working against you. Instead, embrace this new and exciting opportunity you now have to take new actions. This book gives you a new lease on life. Don't miss the opportunity!

One such strategy that hundreds and hundreds and hundreds of our clients have tried … and now swear by … is to build an Automatic Marketing Machine that harnesses the principles of direct response marketing and let the wind work for you instead of pushing so hard against it.

We tell you all this now because it may require some patience from you and some practice to start thinking about your marketing in this new way.

This switch is critical because ...

You've Been Set Up to Struggle Endlessly

As the owner of a small business, you face the constant pressure of having far too much to do and never enough time to get it all done.

If you're not careful, you can get caught in a trap with growing stress from year to year because of the demands coming at you from seemingly every direction—customer attraction; sales; managing production; hiring, training, and managing staff; anticipating and maintaining the physical plant of the business; and financial controls so you don't wind up growing the top line but forget to take anything home from the bottom to feed your family.

It's all an endless challenge—or rather an interrelated set of challenges—that most small business owners simply aren't prepared for. Which is why most of them feel trapped. Because they are trapped.

The way out is by constructing an Automatic Marketing Machine.

To illustrate let's just take a typical example of a very capable small business owner: an attorney running his or her own small law firm.

Let's say this lawyer is ready, willing, and able to work ten hours a day times five days a week times fifty weeks a year. Of course this doesn't mean our hypothetical solo lawyer is actually doing billable work for clients ten hours a day. Instead this very busy but still struggling lawyer probably prioritizes time as follows:

Do whatever legal work they can—maybe four hours a day—because if you don't do the work in front of you, then clients complain, and you starve.

Put out management "fires" in the firm—probably two hours a day.

Get around to sending out some bills—this lawyer probably takes about half an hour per day to account for (make guesses about) the billable work done in between everything else coming at him or her throughout the day.

Meeting with prospective new clients—maybe one to two hours a day—except usually the prospective new clients haven't been prequalified, preeducated, or preconditioned to engage the firm, and so conversion rates are unpredictable, which leads to a lot of demoralizing inefficiency.

Marketing usually happens as an afterthought whenever the well appears to be getting dry—the nonstrategic, unbudgeted, and likely random events of marketing probably average out to about one to two hours a day.

Total: Ten hours a day.

And there you have it: a recipe for burnout from overwork, perpetual unhappiness, and a lifetime of needless financial struggles.

So let's follow the money to examine this last point ...

Let's assume the lawyer from our example bills by the hour and manages to actually collect all four hours a day that he or she bills, times five days, times fifty weeks. That's one thousand hours per year. With a billing rate of $250/hour, this law firm is going to max out at just $250,000 per year, and that assumes all billables are in fact billed and collected, which is unlikely.

And assuming this lawyer is willing or even able to keep up the pace of ten-hour days times five days times fifty weeks, we're still looking at a struggling law firm with an owner who is on the road to burnout. Because working ten hours a day, five days a week, fifty weeks a year is unsustainable and unrealistic.

But let's say there's some superhuman lawyer out there whose family is willing to go along with this sort of plan with no end in sight. After overhead the owner of this firm is still only taking home between $100,000 and $150,000 per year, at least until our superlawyer hits the wall and it all falls apart.

Sadly, there's no end in sight for this lawyer. No escape. No time off. No vacation. No sick days. No leverage. No realistic expectation of sustainability. Life sucks for this lawyer. Life sucks for everyone around this sort of lawyer. And everyone involved pays a price—the lawyer, the family of this lawyer, and the clients, too, because their lawyer isn't showing up as the best version of him- or herself. How could anyone?

Now perhaps you've managed to do better than this. That's great news—congratulations! So now, if your business is already doing better than most, you're probably pretty excited about learning how to build an Automatic Marketing Machine to take your business to even greater heights in terms of revenue, predictability, and freedom for yourself.

On the other hand, if your business has been stuck for more than a few years, at least now you know why and can give yourself a break.

Now you know it likely has nothing to do with your skills or your commitment to your clients and customers.

Once you build your marketing machine, you, too, will soon find you're going to have more free time, better conversion rates with prospective new customers, and more confidence about investing back some of your newfound free time and extra income to build a better business that works for you!

In case you're wondering, here's how the income levels of small business owners tend to spread out in most markets and across most practice areas:

- 1 percent use their business to create tremendous income and wealth,

- 4 percent do very well,

- 15 percent earn a decent living,

- 60 percent struggle endlessly, and

- 20 percent fail.

Yes, it's true. In every market and every industry, there are some entrepreneurs who are using their business to have a much bigger positive impact on the world, and they're creating tremendous income and wealth for themselves, too, in the process. And in those very same cities, in the very same industries, there are some skilled technicians who are presently failing at building their businesses and would gladly take a job if offered.

More to the point, what you've got to know is that nearly 80 percent of the business owners you're going to meet around town are struggling financially and in so many other ways, too, because of the low income and inconsistent revenues of their business, and only 20 percent are actually earning a decent living. This is important for you to know because what passes for normal or acceptable for the vast majority of small business owners doesn't have to be what *you* accept for your standards. You can choose to adopt the standards demanded by the top 5 percent of entrepreneurs. Just don't expect to meet many of them rubbing elbows with everyone else at networking functions … because eagles tend to prefer the company of other eagles.

Not convinced? Here's a test you can carry out by yourself.

Make plans to attend a few different networking events or business discussion groups you can find online, and conduct this test for yourself. Begin by complaining about how tough things are for you in your business. Complain that there aren't enough customers, the customers you do have don't pay enough, and you're working too many hours.

Now, if you were among eagles, they'd either swoop down and try to lift you up or else they'd just fly away to avoid getting trapped. But if you've been to many networking events or waste too much time pecking around with the chickens online, then you already know what results you'll find. Before you know it, you'll be inundated with useless bits of advice, plenty of commiseration, and invitations to join a chorus of stories, rationalizations, and excuses for why things have to be that way.

But that wasn't the test.

This is the test.

Ask any of them to explain their marketing strategy. Ask them to describe, in detail, who their marketing strategy has been designed to resonate with and who it has been equally designed to repel and protect them from.

Ask them what measurements they're using to track ROI and hold their vendors accountable.

Ask about having a marketing budget committed for the next twelve months and financial projections they're basing that budget upon. Ask what the average gross margin is on the services their marketing is designed to sell. Ask if they even know what a gross margin is. Or cost of goods sold.

Ask what KPIs they use to track overall performance of their business or even just the profitability of their marketing. Ask if they have a written business plan that explains in plain English how any of the seven main parts of a successful business are supposed to operate to deliver quality services for customers and profits back to them.

OK, that was RJon, the cofounder and CEO of How to Manage Enterprises, on a bit of a rant with that last paragraph. You can visit HowtoManage.com/MainPartsAMM to learn more about the seven main parts of a successful business.

This book is about the first of the seven main parts: marketing. So, when you conduct your test, just ask the loudest and most persuasive of the complainers to explain to you in plain English what the marketing strategy is for their business, and we're pretty confident we already know what you're going to get.

Part of the problem is that most business owners believe they have to tolerate living the way they are living because that's the way they see that so many other business owners tolerate living their lives too.

Most of them believe they must continue to tolerate living that way because they think the only way out is to advertise and market the way they've seen done by big corporations—so they waste lots of money and time chasing so many different kinds of media to promote image, brand, and presence.

And when that doesn't work, they reach the wrong conclusion about what is or isn't possible instead of the correct conclusion—that they may simply need to find a way to market that is more appropriate for a small business.

You *Need* a Strategy to Separate Yourself from the Competition

The first foundational step you must take in order to attract a steady flow of prospective new customers is developing your answer to the following question:

"Why should a customer choose you and your business versus any and every other option to obtain the very same service to solve the very same problem?"

Your answer to this question is what's known as your unique selling proposition—a.k.a. your USP.

Billion-dollar businesses have been built on the backs of strong USPs. Domino's Pizza became the dominant force in their market through their original, revolutionary USP: *"Fresh, hot pizza delivered in thirty minutes or less, guaranteed."*

Billion-dollar businesses have been built on the backs of strong USPs.

There's a lot to learn from what Domino's did with their USP.

Note that they don't claim to be all things to all people. They're not talking about a "special sauce" or that they use the finest ingredients or that their recipe has been passed down through their family for generations. In fact, they don't speak to the quality of the pizza at all—other than to note that it will still be hot and fresh when they deliver it to you!

They simply make a very clear, appealing, totally unique (at the time) promise to their customers.

What is your USP?

This is going to take a little bit of work. Somewhere in your business, there is a good answer. If not, you need to make one.

There are two different extremes most struggling business owners go to when we start to talk about their unique selling proposition.

First is to jump to the conclusion that there is nothing special about them: "I'm just like all the other businesses in my area who provide basically the same sort of services." The other extreme is to take unwarranted comfort in being better than all the other businesses in town.

Well, sometimes in rare instances, that's true. Maybe your business really is exactly like all the rest. Or maybe you really are the best.

But none of that matters. Because what's going to make your business's marketing more effective isn't bragging about being the best. Everyone is doing that. And when everyone is saying the same thing, it's sort of the same thing as everyone saying nothing. That's why it's not called a best-selling proposition.

Instead, we have to carve out what's going to make your business unique, as in different.

Here are three questions that will help you develop your USP:

- What specifically do you do that's truly unique and different from anyone else in your marketing?

- What unique benefits do you provide to your target market?

- Can you create a unique niche for your services that nobody else can or will?

A lawyer named Carrie Schultz created Men's Rights Divorce out of a "normal" family law firm by creating special programs that cater to the unique challenges of dads who need to file or respond to a divorce. Admittedly, 80 percent of what Carrie's firm does is the same as what would be called for if representing a mother going through a divorce or even a man or a woman with no children. But if you're a father facing the prospect of divorce, the 20 percent difference could make

100 percent of the difference, and so more than two million dollars' worth of business is now attracted to Carrie's law firm every year.

RJon's firm manages hundreds of entrepreneurs with an impressive track record of growth, and so it is with much experience that we say there's no need to allow your business to be perceived by the market as being like every other business, only better—or, worse, cheaper. Take the time to create your own USP—it's one of the greatest marketing weapons you can ever have for your business.

The Legend of John Henry

You might find yourself wondering …

"I'm already working events, getting referrals, and getting clients and customers on my own. Why would I need to build an Automatic Marketing Machine?"

Consider the legend of John Henry—a story about a man in the 1800s whose prowess with the railroad hammer made him a legend.

John Henry could swing a hammer like no one else. He could drive a railroad spike with one massive swing of the hammer and drive more spikes straight into the ground in an hour than anyone else could.

John Henry was a big, muscular hammer swinger, and everyone admired him greatly because of how much work he could do in an hour—just like everyone may admire you today in your business or in your peer group because of how much capacity for work you have. And how much work you can produce in an hour. And how many customers and clients you can produce in an hour of networking, or speechmaking, or posting on social media.

You can swing a hammer like nobody else!

Well, we're here to tell you that the age of the hammer swinger is over because someone invented a steam hammer.

And it worked like this: a steam hammer would get rolled down the track from spike to spike. A lever would get pulled or a button pushed, and boom, boom, boom, the machine would drive a steel spike into the ground. Almost as fast as John Henry could with just one of his mighty swings!

One day, as legend has it, a competition was organized, John Henry versus the steam hammer, to see who could get farther in a day.

You know who won?

John Henry won because John Henry is a legend!

Your marketing skills may be the stuff of legend too. You may be better than anyone at getting new customers and clients. Maybe you get all the business you do because of how great you are.

The only problem is at the end of the day, John Henry dropped dead of a heart attack with a hammer in his hand, just like maybe you're going to drop dead of a heart attack because all customer acquisition depends on how great you are.

Now get this …

A mediocre marketing machine will outperform the most brilliant marketer in the world **every time.**

This book will get you out of the railroad tunnel, get you out of the role of hammer swinger, and help you build an Automatic Marketing Machine that will keep doing the marketing for you day in and day out, week in and week out, month in and month out.

You want to go on vacation? No problem. The machine is going to keep chugging along. You get sick? No problem. The machine is going to keep chugging along. A loved one needs you to come to their aid, and you'll never forgive yourself if you can't be there for him or her? No problem. The marketing machine is going to keep chugging along.

That's what your machine can do for you.

Use of the word *transformative* would not be an overstatement.

WARNING: Chances are, your thinking about how you want to be marketing your business and living your life has already begun to change.

As we continue to explain and reveal the blueprint, there's a very good chance you're going to experience a quantum leap in terms of how you think about every part of how you manage your business.

As much as we'd love it if you'd immediately run out and tell everyone you know about these concepts, please don't do that just yet. Because they won't understand. And you won't have the proof you may need to withstand the onslaught of doubts and criticism you'll likely encounter when you share new ideas that challenge the beliefs that so many (struggling) small business owners have about how to market their business.

Instead, give yourself a chance to build a marketing machine for your own business and let it begin producing amazing results for you. Then you won't have to explain or defend as much to the entrepreneurs you're trying to help.

And then we'll have a *different* conversation about why most of them will *still* ignore what you say and keep repeating what's not currently working out very well for them and never will.

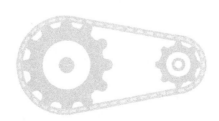

CHAPTER TWO

DO YOUR MARKETING VENDORS HAVE YOU CARRYING WATER?

I (Danny) grew up in Africa. When I was five years old, my parents moved from Minneapolis, Minnesota, across the Atlantic Ocean to Liberia, a small country on the West African coast.

If this sounds like a dramatic move today, trust me, it was even more dramatic back in 1989—before email, before cell phones, before even the internet was available to most people. Moving to West Africa under those circumstances meant telling friends and family back home, "Goodbye—talk to you in a few years."

My parents moved to join a mission organization—a group that built hospitals, dental clinics, schools, and orphanages among some of the neediest people and groups in the world.

Even as a five-year-old, you can't spend much time in Africa without recognizing that many, many families live in extreme poverty.

And one very significant reason why so many people live in poverty is that countless villages across the African continent don't have easy access to fresh, clean water for drinking, cleaning, cooking, or bathing.

So, by necessity, millions of women across the continent spend most of their waking hours walking from their village to the closest source of water, filling up five-gallon buckets, and then carrying those buckets full of water home to meet their families' daily needs.

And then doing it again. And again. And again.

Many women spend eight to ten hours *every single day* gathering water—walking several miles to a clean source of water, filling up their buckets, and walking back home. And then turning around to do it again. It's a manual, labor-intensive task, and it takes up most of their time each day.

UNICEF calculates that, worldwide, women and girls spend about <u>two hundred million hours every single day</u> collecting water.

Two hundred million hours per day, 1.4 billion hours per week, 6 billion hours per month, 72 billion hours per year.

It's a tragic waste of time.

This represents billions of hours of productivity and innovation that <u>doesn't happen</u> each year—because women are forced to spend their time in a manual, menial, labor-intensive process just to meet the most basic needs for themselves and their families.

That's half the workforce carrying buckets of water instead of carrying on with more productive work. They're trying to break out of poverty, but they're doing it with one hand tied behind their backs.

It's a huge problem.

Which is why there are many nonprofit and governmental organizations focused on solving this problem, village by village by village.

They do this in lots of different ways:

- digging wells

- creating rain catchment tanks

- building dams to create strategically located water basins

- installing water pumps and pipes to transport water back to the villages

Ultimately the dream is for every child in every village to grow up in a home where having a reliable source of clean running water for cooking, cleaning, and bathing becomes their new normal.

Most of this technology is extremely low tech and would not be impressive at all to those of us who grew up in a first-world country with easy access to water simply by turning on a faucet. In fact, once you know what you know, it's all so ... obvious. And profitable too!

"Well, if it's all so obvious and low tech, then why don't they just invest a little time to dig some wells, create a rain catchment system, etc., etc.? Are they dumb or something?"

Having lived in Africa for many years, I can assure you that the intelligence of the average person who considers it normal to devote half their family's productive capacity to carrying buckets of water is on par with the intelligence of the average American. It's not a matter of intelligence. It's a matter of awareness. They're understandably unaware of how much better life could be ... and that is why they don't devote the time, energy, and resources to create a reliable system for bringing fresh, clean water to their villages and homes, automatically.

You are probably a person of above average intelligence. Yet from the perspective of someone who has already built and now enjoys the benefits of having an Automatic Marketing Machine that brings regular, consistent new prospects to their business like turning on a faucet ... from this perspective, you're in the same trap, burning half your time and energy lugging buckets of water back to your business to keep it alive.

Can you just imagine what it would mean for a family to go from living day by day, dependent on manual labor for their water supply … to having a faucet in their home!

All of a sudden, instead of burning most of her day walking back and forth to gather water, a woman could invest her time and energy more productively. For example, she could now

- plant a crop to lift her family out of food insecurity,

- take some of that extra food production to market, eventually saving up enough capital to invest in a donkey and then using the donkey to pull a plow, which would increase crop yields pretty dramatically with significantly less manual labor,

- use the increased crop yield, more food security, and hard currency coming into the household, along with the extra time not spent transporting water, manually plowing a field, or recovering from physical exhaustion, to make formal education a real possibility, and

- use that education, some extra income, and food security to enter the workforce, start a small business, or simply enjoy the benefits of the standard of living you probably already take for granted, which includes time for rest, recreation, and planning for a better future.

That's a really big deal.

You know what else could be a really big deal?

It could be a really big deal if you could go from waking up every morning at the crack of dawn so you can head down to the river with your five-gallon buckets to lug some prospective new customers back to your office in order to keep your business and your family alive.

Can you just imagine what a transformation it would be for that family living in a remote African village to wake up six months from now and have the benefits of reliable clean water merely by turning on a faucet?

Can you just imagine what a transformation it would be for your own family to wake up six months from now and have the benefits of a reliable and predictable stream of prospective new clients to your business because you followed the instructions contained in this book and built an Automatic Marketing Machine for your business?

If this is all so obvious, then why doesn't every small business owner create an Automatic Marketing Machine of their very own?

Like the human body needs water, your business requires a steady flow of new prospects in order to survive and grow. Humans can't last more than a week or two without water, and your business won't last much longer without a flow of new prospects.

You probably thought we were going to say new *customers*, didn't you?

But in reality, *prospective* new customers—the *right kind* of prospective new customers—are even more important to the long-term health of your business than are actual paying customers. This is because having a steady and reliable flow of new *prospects* empowers you to be <u>selective</u>.

Just imagine what would happen if the next time you lug your buckets of water all the way back from the river, you find a dead fish in the bottom of the bucket.

If your only choices are to make the best of it, tell your family there's no water today, or walk all the way back to the river ... if we're being completely

Having a steady and reliable flow of new *prospects* empowers you to be <u>selective</u>.

honest, what choice do you already know most small business owners are probably going to make?

So, yes, ultimately your business needs new customers to make payroll, cover rent, and give your family a profit, but your sanity requires standards be kept, and it's a lot easier to keep your standards when you can turn on a faucet and bring more prospects to choose from. When you can do this, it just completely transforms (for the better) the relationship between your business and its customers. This is the kind of new normal we wrote this book to help you create. It's how thousands of our own clients are already living. And we want nothing less for you and your family too.

"But guys, if this is all so obvious, then why doesn't every small business owner create an Automatic Marketing Machine?"

The answer isn't because they're stupid.

Instead, it's because they just don't know how much better their life could be. So they don't go out in search of a better way. Which is why they don't wind up reading books like this to educate themselves about how to do it.

Like we said, the truth will set you free.

But first it will piss you off!

It really is this simple.

CHAPTER THREE

YES, THIS STUFF REALLY WORKS!

W e'll assume, given that you're reading this book, you understand marketing is important for your business. Great businesses that don't have any customers have merely the potential to be great businesses. And great business owners who accept bad customers because they're desperate to find where the next one will come from— well, they just end up miserable.

So our purpose in writing this book is *not* to persuade you that marketing is important for the health of your business. You already know that, or you wouldn't be reading this book. Instead, our purpose is to give you a vision for a better way to think about the marketing of your business overall.

Because once you have that vision firmly in mind, we can give you the blueprint for how to build an Automatic Marketing Machine of your very own. One that operates on your behalf, 24-7, 365 days per year, whether you're in the office, at home with your family, or on vacation. With a clear vision of how much better every aspect of your life could be then, we know you'll do something about it!

On the surface it may seem that this book is meant to help you create an Automatic Marketing *Machine* that fuels the growth of your business—so that you don't get stuck in a manual, tedious, time-consuming *job*.

But what this book is *really* about is helping you capture and keep a vision of a better life so that you get busy turning that vision into your new reality.

And we understand you may be a bit skeptical at this point. After all, we just finished saying that your whole business and your whole quality of life can be quickly transformed for relatively little money.

You may have been going down to the river with your buckets for years or even decades. It's a familiar if unpleasant routine. You've probably developed lots of stories and gathered plenty of evidence for why it has to be that way. Most of the business owners you know go down to the river every morning with their buckets too. That may even be how you met them, all down at the river together, trading tips on the best way to carry a five-gallon bucket full of water on your head!

And here we are telling you it doesn't have to be this way! Instead, things could be so much better for you.

Blasphemy!

It sounds too good to be true!

Don't worry. We get it. And we don't blame you for being skeptical. There is just so much BS out there today—so many self-proclaimed experts, so many marketers making so many unfulfilled promises, so many "coaches" and "consultants" selling bright, shiny objects that sound really amazing but don't actually do anything for you.

So no, we don't blame you at all for being skeptical.

Instead, we want you to become a true believer. Because you have to believe that there is a better way to live, a better way to run your business, a better normal available for you and your family. Or else you're not going to put down your bucket and pick up the tools we're going to give you in this book to build a better life.

So please keep an open mind, and allow us to help you become a true believer.

Need more proof? Flip to the final chapter of this book—or, better yet, point the camera of your smartphone at this QR code—and set aside a few hours because we've got more proof that this works ... that this is actually working ... than you probably have time to watch, listen to, or read about!

"From Struggle and Stress to Total Freedom and Peace of Mind"

Seth Greene is a financial planner, and he started his career working with a big national financial services company. When the financial bubble burst in 2007, he hung out his own shingle. He found himself struggling to stand out in a crowded industry. He spent a lot of time doing the same things that other financial planners were doing—like going to networking events and making cold calls with next to nothing to show for it. He was tired of hauling leaky buckets back and forth from the river, and he knew there had to be a better way.

So he began studying marketing. He discovered the principles of direct response marketing, devoured all the information he could find, and started to implement what he learned.

His first order of business was to develop a unique selling proposition so that he could stand out from all the other financial planners in his market. And to do that, he niched down his practice to specialize in providing financial planning services specifically to help parents figure out how to pay for their kids' college education.

He got crystal clear on who his ideal prospects are—affluent suburban parents who have really smart, overachieving kids who want to go to top private universities but think they can't afford it and therefore think they have to settle for attending a state school.

And then he created a powerful USP: "We'll help you get your kid to an elite private school for less than the cost of a state school."

With this foundational work done, he started to plan his first lead generation campaigns—which you'll learn about in chapters 9 and 10—and he began building his Automatic Marketing Machine. He started with very simple, primitive systems, like old-fashioned direct mail and email marketing. And he started offering webinars and seminars specifically for high school guidance counselors— who are in the perfect position to refer him clients—and began to create drip campaigns to keep them engaged and keep his firm top of mind. He launched a website built around his USP—www. HowToFindMoneyForCollege.com—and created lead magnets and lead-nurture campaigns to fill his pipeline with ideal prospects.

The results were stunning, even to Seth. After years of hauling leaky buckets—struggling to stand out and attract qualified prospects—all of a sudden he had a marketing system that was filling his pipeline for him. His firm began to grow dramatically—he tripled revenues, then tripled them again the next year. Over a period of five years, his average revenue growth was over 1,500 percent. Today, Seth has a robust marketing machine in place, feeding his sales team a steady supply of qualified, preconditioned prospects that are already predisposed to do business with him.

Because of the confidence he has in his marketing machine, Seth has been able to invest in building his team and scaling his business. He now enjoys the freedom, peace of mind, and financial rewards that only an Automatic Marketing Machine can provide.

"Nothing Moved the Needle until He Jumped Down the Rabbit Hole"

Francisco Sirvent started his law firm in 2007 as a way to provide his family with a better life by helping other people with the big problems in their lives—estate planning, asset protection, elder law, probate, and related litigation.

Their best clients are couples within two to three years of retirement who have a net worth of a million dollars. Usually, they come from white-collar professions (teachers, engineers, lawyers, accountants).

Francisco started in 2007 with nothing—no book of business, no network, no referral sources. And, worst of all, no one who had the answers. Other lawyers offered plenty of advice, "but it never seemed to create momentum."

The firm grossed between $80,000 and $100,000 per year for the first four years, and Francisco was able to support his growing family (a wife and four young children at that time) only by keeping overhead extremely low and pinching pennies everywhere possible.

Francisco attended networking meetings. Found introductions to financial advisors, hundreds of them, to build relationships. Used software to create automation, and attended plenty of CLEs and bar functions.

Nothing helped. Nothing moved the needle.

The struggle cost him six years of his life. While his kids were cute and tiny, he was scrambling, working eighty-plus hours per week to be the attorney, receptionist, secretary, paralegal, and office manager. His wife got too little attention. They couldn't and didn't take the vacations they wanted, they couldn't save toward retirement, they accumulated debt—Francisco came to the brink of losing all hope of a better life.

Then Francisco engaged one of RJon's businesses, How to Manage a Small Law Firm, to help him grow and manage his business. One of the first things they did was help him overhaul his marketing. "I printed out your ten foundational rules and put them everywhere—my desk, my laptop, my phone." He decided to jump down the rabbit hole and started offering a free public seminar about estate planning. "That first seminar was the first time I'd ever set ten appointments in one day, and we haven't looked back since!"

Francisco was hooked from that point on.

The first year he used this type of marketing was 2013/2014, and Francisco's firm grossed more than $200,000, more than doubling its best previous year. And they've been growing every year since. In 2019 Keystone Law grossed $1.4 million, and with help from RJon's team, the net was the highest it's ever been. By creating an Automatic Marketing Machine, Francisco's firm has been able to help fourteen times more clients than before, and that's enabled Francisco to build a custom dream house from scratch, propelled him to hire a professional firm administrator (chief operating officer) for the first time, and at last, the law firm is becoming less of a job and transforming into a business that isn't dependent on him.

"My Marketing Machine Drives Revenue So I Can Enjoy My Life!"

Frank Bravata's business, Cyber Brigade, provides IT services to businesses with ten to fifty employees, with a special focus on professional services firms.

He wasn't always an entrepreneur—in fact, he kind of "fell into it" when he was laid off from his IT job in 2009.

Frank knew that he was a skilled IT technician. But he didn't know—and in fact he didn't know that he didn't know—anything about marketing. And so, predictably, Frank struggled to attract clients, and his business was stalled. He put time and money into brand-style marketing, like some of his competitors were doing, but nothing really worked to generate new clients.

Everything changed for him when he discovered direct response marketing. Frank embraced the concept that all his marketing needed to be trackable and measurable. That all his marketing needed to include a strong call to action. That he needed to demand a positive ROI on every dollar he spends on marketing. He began to look at his marketing like a vending machine—"If I put a dollar in, I better get at least two dollars out."

Frank began building an Automatic Marketing Machine. He created simple lead magnets to generate prospects and lead-nurture campaigns to preeducate his prospects before he let them schedule a sales call. He built automated follow-up systems so that even if a prospect didn't sign on the dotted line to become a client, Frank's business stayed top of mind for months and even years after the first interaction.

With his marketing machine in place, Frank has seen steady, predictable revenue growth. He's grown his business by *at least* 25 percent every single year for the past nine years. And because his revenue growth is predictable, Frank knows when it's time to hire and when it's time to invest in his growing infrastructure. He's even launched a new division of his business focused on cybersecurity for solopreneurs and high-net-worth individuals (www.EntreGuard.com).

And perhaps best of all, these days Frank is working only twenty to thirty hours per week because he's not wasting his time lugging buckets back and forth from the river. He doesn't have to hustle and chase down bad leads anymore. His Automatic Marketing Machine has given him the freedom to spend his time how he wants to, and he's free to enjoy life on his own terms.

For many, many more stories and case studies, flip to the back of this book. And then scan the QR code or visit www.AutomaticMarketingMachine.com/CaseStudies for even *more* case studies of successful entrepreneurs who have built Automatic Marketing Machines for their businesses. Yes—this stuff really works.

The Proof Is in the Pudding

There are so many "gurus" these days that it can be hard to know who to trust. If you feel overwhelmed with the conflicting advice and ideas you see, we don't blame you.

As they say, **the proof is in the pudding**. And we want you to know you can rely on the principles in this book to help you build not only a better business but, ultimately, a better life.

These stories represent just the tip of the iceberg of the lives changed—thousands of entrepreneurs who now feel empowered by the education-based marketing that's at the center of the Automatic Marketing Machine.

Even more exciting, assuming the average small business helps just one hundred customers per year to

> **Life is just better when you can rely on your Automatic Marketing Machine.**

have a better life or a better business of their own … that's hundreds of thousands of households that are better off because of the businesses that are benefitting too!

Life is just different—better—when you can rely upon an Automatic Marketing Machine instead of your businesses' financial viability being dependent on your manual labor, carrying buckets.

So no matter when you are holding this book in your hands (or maybe technology has allowed it to be beamed directly into your brain by now), you can have confidence that the principles and strategies described in this book are reliable and timeless. And if you'll invest the time to build it, your Automatic Marketing Machine will continue to serve you for years to come—attracting slam-dunk prospects to your business.

CHAPTER FOUR

WHY MOST SMALL BUSINESS MARKETING DOESN'T WORK ... AND WHAT TO DO ABOUT IT

"The person who follows the crowd will usually go no further than the crowd. The person who walks alone is likely to find himself in places no one has ever seen before."

—ALBERT EINSTEIN

W e wrote this book to teach you how to build your Automatic Marketing Machine—how to create a steady, consistent, predictable stream of new prospects into your business. And to do it all without having to be lugging buckets back and forth from the river.

But really, we wrote this book to unlock the productive human potential that's trapped inside of so many entrepreneurs who are busy lugging water instead of making people's lives and businesses better.

You should know ahead of time, though, that your Automatic Marketing Machine isn't going to look like most of the marketing that you see all around you. Your marketing isn't going to fit in with what passes for marketing for so many struggling small businesses.

You need to be prepared to do things differently if you're going to get different results. And the principles we're going to introduce in this book will definitely seem different. They may even seem radical. That's because they are radical and they are different.

But they're radically different for a very good reason. The concepts taught in this book will seem radically different from most small business marketing you see all around you because **most small business marketing is flat-out terrible!**

And by terrible, we mean just one thing: <u>it does not work</u>.

Hang on. We'll explain exactly why it doesn't work soon enough. But first we need to be sure we're all speaking the same language. And to do that we're going to do something most so-called marketing gurus desperately want you *not* to do. We're going to define some criteria.

So let's define arguably the *most important word* you'll use as the responsible manager of your marketing budget. The word is *work*. As in "Is this working?" and "Is this working well enough to justify additional expenditures on it?" and "Gee, I'm beginning to get the feeling that my marketing agency doesn't want me to know if my marketing is actually working for my business!"

This is the only standard you should have for your marketing, don't you agree?

Does it work?

Does it bring me enough prospects so that I can feel confident about being selective?

Does it bring me enough customers (but not too many) to keep my business working at or close to 100 percent capacity?

Does it bring me only the right kinds of prospects to protect me and my staff from having to waste our time with everyone else?

Does my marketing produce a positive ROI?

How do I know?

To say your business's marketing works, you must be able to answer yes to all these questions but the last one. And for the last one, you have to be able to show proof.

If you'll follow the steps we're going to lay out for you in this book, you'll be able to build your own Automatic Marketing Machine practically for free. It might not be the prettiest thing in the world. But pretty isn't what matters. What matters is: Does it work? And it will.

Eventually you'll want to reinvest some of your additional profits to hire a marketing agency. But you don't have to do that right away. In fact, we recommend that you build at least a basic prototype yourself so that you can understand from experience why and how it works.

This way you'll be able to recognize when that fancy marketing agency with the fancy office and the fancy name doesn't understand why or how this stuff works. Because, as we're about to explain, most don't. And worse yet, they have a vested interest in being sure you don't either!

But by following the steps we're going to lay out for you in this book, you'll become an empowered consumer and never be held hostage by the bucket sellers who don't want you to be smart enough to ask the most fundamental question there is in all marketing: Is it working?

Look, when we say most small business marketing is flat-out terrible, we're not just spinning hyperbole. We're not just throwing rocks at other agencies, "gurus," and coaches. And we're not trying to hurt anyone's feelings. What we are saying is that most marketing is terrible when evaluated using the same objective criteria we insist our own clients use when evaluating our work for them: Is it working?

Sadly, huge amounts of money are wasted, month after month after month, by entrepreneurs and marketing agencies that don't know what they're doing—or don't care enough to do better. So if you consider the marketing produced by most businesses and most marketing agencies as an indicator of what *you* should be doing, then you will be doomed to repeat their mistakes. They'll have you lugging buckets of water the rest of your life because they're in the business of selling you the buckets!

Remember, if you're looking for a marketing vendor that won't have you hauling buckets, make sure you visit www.AutomaticMarketingMachine.com/vendors for a list of certified vendors who have been carefully vetted by our team. Or just scan the QR code below:

The Top Ten Reasons Why Most Small Business Marketing Doesn't Work

1. Most small businesses are unclear about the purpose of marketing … and their marketing agencies like it this way! Ask your average business owner why marketing is important, and you'll get answers like:

- "To get our name out there"

- "To look more credible"

- "To impress my family and friends" (they won't say this, but they're thinking it)

- "To show up first on Google"

- "Everyone else is doing it"

Wrong, wrong, wrong, wrong, and wrong.

The sole and express purpose of marketing is this:

To deliver prospective new customers to the front door of your businesses, already prequalified, already predisposed to hire your business, and all at the right time and in the right quantity to keep your business operating at full capacity but not so much that your staff burns out and customers become dissatisfied due to poor service, which naturally happens when you're overloaded.

That's it.

The purpose of your marketing is to generate qualified leads for your business. To bring qualified leads to your business so that your sales team can convert them into paying customers.

Credibility, brand awareness, search engine rankings … all those are secondary considerations.

Credibility is valuable only to the extent to which it helps you generate qualified leads.

Brand awareness is valuable only to the extent to which it helps you generate qualified leads.

Credibility and brand awareness are a means to your end. The smartest marketers with the most successful businesses don't allow their egos to convince them that credibility or brand awareness is the end in itself.

Google rankings are valuable only to the extent that they help your business generate qualified leads.

"Is it working?"

Never allow yourself to be seduced into believing anything else in marketing really matters. At least not for a small business. Clarity around this empowers you to evaluate your marketing, interview and hire the right marketing vendors, and then hold them accountable. "How are we going to measure whether and how well it's working?" This single question will allow you to see through the charlatans, scam artists, and well-intentioned fools who would otherwise take your money and trade it for pretty graphics and vanity metrics that don't really matter.

2. Most small businesses engage in random acts of marketing rather than building a system. For most small business owners, marketing is a completely manual process. Marketing usually consists of an entrepreneur attending networking events, schmoozing with referral sources, or making the occasional post on Facebook or LinkedIn.

Lugging their buckets to the river each morning.

And while these tactics can work reasonably well, they're entirely dependent on the time, interest, and ability of the business owner who's executing them.

Which means that, inevitably, there is a lot of stopping and starting with these initiatives.

Think about this for a minute:

If all the bucket carrying works, great, now you have a bunch of customers to serve. That's good, right? Except now who is going to do the manual labor to ensure that there are plenty of customers to serve next month? And the month after that? This on-again, off-again pattern of marketing sets up a cascading effect of feast or famine that only gets worse and worse the more effectively the manual bucket-hauling method of marketing works.

Think about this for a minute. The cure is actually contributing to the disease!

Because what do you think happens during times of feast? Businesses get sloppy with follow-up and often fail to maximize the value of every dollar spent on marketing. Why watch the pennies? After all, we have plenty!

And what do you think happens during times of famine? Businesses get desperate and accept cases they know they ought not accept from customers they know they're going to wish they didn't accept work from.

Next thing you know, the owner is burned out, the staff is unhappy, and the business is in a cash crunch. Which only puts even *more* pressure on the entrepreneur without the Automatic Marketing Machine to run back down to the river and bring back any water that's available ... even if it's not the best-quality water.

Committing random acts of marketing is no way to build your business or live your life!

Instead, you need a system that operates without your day-to-day attention so you can bring some sanity back into your life.

3. Most small businesses market their services to anyone and everyone rather than to a clearly defined target market. Effective, profitable marketing campaigns are laser focused on the *specific* audience they're targeting. Effective campaigns are laser focused on the *specific* problem they're addressing. The best marketing campaigns take a sniper approach rather than a shotgun approach—which allows for maximum efficiency and therefore maximum profitability. This is a concept that we will discuss in great detail later in this book.

Most businesses take the opposite approach with their marketing. They're so starved for new customers that they become afraid of losing even the tiniest opportunity. So they attempt to be *everything* to *everyone*. Which of course makes their marketing very compelling to no one.

An example is the law firm that practices door law—i.e., rather than focusing on a specific practice area, they'll accept any client who walks through the door with practically any kind of case or matter—whether it's a criminal case, a slip-and-fall accident, or even creating an estate plan. This leads to many problems from an operational perspective, which we don't have space to cover in this book. (But you can visit www.HowToManage.com/AMM to learn why this is such a huge operational problem and what you can do to fix it.) It also leads to many problems from a marketing perspective—most notably bland, generic, *boring* marketing that doesn't excite *anyone* because it's attempting to appease *everyone*.

Focusing your marketing on a specific problem—or a small group of related problems typically faced by a specific type of customer—is an important first step. We know it's counterintuitive, but this approach really is far more profitable, as it allows even a very small business to create marketing campaigns that are laser focused and therefore highly relevant to a specific target market.

4. Most businesses communicate the wrong messages in their marketing. Businesses exist to solve problems for their customers to help them have a better future. Every single day, all across the country, in big cities and small towns, businesses are helping their customers to protect themselves, protect their families, and take advantage of opportunities so that ultimately they can have a better future.

Customers engage your business when they have a specific *problem* or a specific *opportunity* that they need help addressing **so they can have a better future**.

If you think about it, the reason you're reading this book right now is because you want to have a better future and you are smart enough to know that having an Automatic Marketing Machine for your business can help you have that better future.

So when an entrepreneur is marketing their business, the messaging should speak to the problems and opportunities that target prospects are experiencing in their lives and paint a picture of the better future that the business can help its customers achieve.

But ... that's not what most businesses are doing. Most small business marketing messages are myopically focused on themselves ... their years of experience, the awards they've won, their impressive office space, and so forth. It's all about *them*.

This approach is completely wrong, and it's an easy way to guarantee that your marketing will fall flat on its face.

5. Most small business marketing asks prospects to take the wrong first step. Here's the classic situation. Maybe you can relate?

A business—let's say a family law firm—spends a bunch of money on Google Ads and drives prospects to their website.

Hooray!

The website says something to the effect of "Quick, call this number or fill out this form to schedule an appointment." There's no prequalification, prescreening, or preeducation.

The prospect dutifully responds and picks up the phone to schedule an appointment.

Hooray!

The prospect schedules the appointment for 4:00 p.m. on a Wednesday.

At 6:00 p.m. that Wednesday, the law firm owner has a date to take their spouse out for a nice dinner.

Wednesday rolls around, and the prospect shows up at the office at 4:00 p.m.

Hooray!

This family law firm has a unique and compelling passion for representing people who put their family first and are reasonable, rational people who are unfortunately going through a divorce—and who believe they want to make a decision today that they'll be proud of when they go to their child's graduation in ten or fifteen years.

And so they're not going to spend thousands and thousands of dollars fighting over the toaster and making stupid decisions now that they're going to regret in the future.

That's the mission of the law firm, and those are the types of clients that the law firm wants to serve.

But because the law firm's website doesn't have any type of preeducation or prescreening information, the client who is now showing up at the office is *exactly the opposite of the type of client the law firm wants*, and this quickly becomes clear during the consultation.

Now the prospect is in a very bad mood because they've just wasted a whole bunch of time—they left work early, got dressed up, drove across town, and dealt with parking in an unfamiliar area, hoping that this law firm was going to help their life get better.

So they start peppering the lawyer with question after question that woulda, shoulda, coulda been addressed with proper prescreening and preeducation materials on the website.

Time keeps ticking away … 4:30 p.m. … 5:00 p.m. … and now the lawyer is anxious and uptight because they know they're going to be late for their date, and they're even more anxious because they know when they get home, they're going to be in a bad mood because they just spent an hour going around and around in circles with the wrong type of client.

As a result, everyone is frustrated, everyone is disappointed, and everyone has wasted their time.

By the way, it's not that this client is the wrong type of client for every law firm—it's just that this specific law firm isn't the right law firm for this client. As a result, everyone is frustrated, everyone is disappointed, and everyone has wasted their time.

So when the lawyer gets home—late—and not in a good mood, and their spouse says "I'm sorry you're late, but I understand that you were working hard for us," the lawyer has to lie and say, "Yes, I was doing this so we could all have a better life," because he can't admit the truth, which is, "I was just wasting my time meeting with somebody that I never should have been meeting with, and now everyone is unhappy."

That's what happens when marketing asks prospects to take the wrong first step. Later in this book you'll learn what the *right* first step actually is.

6. Most small businesses try to emulate Fortune 500 businesses in their marketing. It's understandable that small business owners would try to emulate the advertising they see every time they turn on the TV.

But billion-dollar businesses can afford to spend millions of dollars per year on this type of brand awareness advertising. And who knows, maybe they have the KPIs to show that brand building eventually gives them a great ROI.

But we have seen too many small business owners go broke and ruin what has the very real potential to be a multimillion- or even a ten-million- or twenty-million-dollar business trying to do what no one should even be thinking about doing unless they've got millions of dollars to spend on mere brand awareness.

We've all seen it—beautiful, polished ads, on TV for thirty seconds, that cost more to produce and display than most small businesses will generate in revenue over an entire year.

In 2019 Samsung spent more than $2 billion on advertising.

AT&T spent over $3 billion on advertising.

And Coca-Cola spent more than $4 *billion* on advertising!

As a small business, you just can't keep up, and you shouldn't try.

Big businesses may have the wherewithal to invest tens of millions of dollars to build brand awareness over many years in hope that when a prospect finally gets around to going out to shop for whatever it is the brand stands for, that brand awareness will tip the scales and cause the prospect to give the big company their business.

But this takes more years to work than you have time to wait. And it puts more tens of millions of dollars at risk than you can afford to gamble. And as far as we are concerned, the worst part of this big long gamble on brand-awareness advertising is that it is almost impossible to track or measure ROI, which is another way of saying that marketing vendors who don't want to be held accountable for anything *love it*!

So it's understandable why some of your peers who have never heard of direct response marketing and don't know any better than to pour their money into untrackable, untestable, unmeasurable, long-term, "Let's hope this works eventually" brand building ... it's understandable why those peers of yours would unwittingly model what they see those big companies doing every day, wrongly thinking, "If it works for them, it's gotta work for us too."

Emulating Fortune 500 businesses with your marketing is a recipe for disaster.

7. Most businesses hire the wrong marketing vendors. Most marketing vendors have a very different set of priorities than their clients do. You, as the client of a marketing agency, hire that agency for the purpose of acquiring more prospects, more customers, and more revenue for your business. That's why you're doing it!

But the average marketing agency's priority list looks more like this:

Get paid.

Get more clients (for themselves).

Win awards.

Build their reputation.

Grow their staff.

Upgrade office space.

And then somewhere near the bottom of their list is ensuring that their campaigns are actually producing results for their clients.

Which is why the average marketing agency is good at winning new clients for *themselves*, and good at creating websites and marketing materials that *look nice*, and very, very good at making excuses for poor performance so that their clients (victims) keep paying them ... and not always so great at actually producing results for their clients.

Meanwhile most entrepreneurs have never been taught how to properly identify, hire, and manage marketing vendors … because they didn't teach *that* skill in business school.

And it's important that you know that there are virtually no barriers to entry for anyone who wants to call themselves a marketing professional. No degree is required, no license need be obtained, no exams must be passed. All that it takes to start a "marketing agency" is a laptop, a cell phone, a cursory knowledge of industry buzzwords, and a few unsuspecting victims willing to write a check each month.

All of the above creates a perfect storm for waste, failure, and abuse—and makes it very easy to understand *why* so many small businesses are led astray by their marketing agencies.

The good news for you, our listener, is that we have devoted an entire chapter of this book to the process of hiring and managing your marketing vendors. And of course you can visit www.AutomaticMarketingMachine.com/vendors for a directory of vetted, certified agencies.

8. Most small businesses do not track and measure their marketing performance. You should not spend a dollar—not one single dollar—on a marketing campaign in which you haven't clearly defined your objectives and your criteria for judging success.

Every single marketing campaign *must* have a defined objective and predetermined KPIs *before* you commit to launching it.

The ultimate measure of campaign effectiveness, as we've discussed above, is the number of qualified prospects generated for your business divided by the cost of the campaign. This gives you a cost per qualified prospect, which is the single most important metric for any ad campaign.

But some campaigns may take a little while to ramp up and begin producing prospects, and so it's important that you've defined other metrics to help you assess whether or not the campaign is on track.

For example, with a digital campaign, you'd likely track impressions, cost per impression, reach, click-through rate, cost per click, etc.

(By the way, you can scan the QR code below or visit www.AutomaticMarketingMachine.com/KPIs to download a simple template to track KPIs for your marketing campaigns. Download the template, and then send it to your marketing vendor and ask that they fill in the KPIs and send the report to you at least once per month. This simple tool alone is worth the price of this book one thousand times over … if you use it!)

Most small businesses don't track *any* of this. There's no tracking, and there's no accountability. And by the time they realize that their marketing agency is no good or that their latest campaign was a total miss, they've blown tens of thousands of dollars that they'll never recover.

Please recognize that your marketing agency is *not* going to volunteer for this level of transparency and accountability. *You* have to demand it from them. It's your responsibility to ensure every dollar spent is tracked and measured—and you can't take no for an answer.

9. Most small businesses do not build follow-up systems. The money is in the follow-up. Fortunes are won through follow-up.

Successful, profitable marketing systems are built around follow-up. Your Automatic Marketing Machine will be built around follow-up.

Follow up with new prospects who've just contacted your business.

Follow up with old leads that have gone cold.

Follow up with prospects who have completed their initial consultation but not yet signed on the dotted line.

Follow up with past clients and customers.

Follow up with referral sources.

Follow up, follow up, follow up.

Why? Because, simply put, we humans in the twenty-first century are incredibly distracted and incredibly busy. The human brain is bombarded with somewhere between ten thousand and fifty thousand distinct thoughts every single day. And so you're sadly mistaken if you think that prospects, customers, and referral sources are going to remember you if you're not proactively staying in touch with them.

To stay relevant and engaged with your prospects—which is essential if they are going to hire you and/or refer to you—you have to follow up with them proactively.

And because you are likely to have thousands or even tens of thousands of new prospects, old prospects, new customers, old customers, and referral sources—each of whom need to be followed up with dozens of times in a calendar year—you cannot possibly keep up without building a *system* that runs automatically. By the time you're done reading this book, you'll understand how to do this.

Most small businesses don't have a follow-up system in place—and consequently, most of them are squandering massive opportunity month after month.

10. Most small businesses confuse marketing and sales. There are *seven main parts of a successful business*. There are also *seven main parts of a struggling business*. The difference between the successful businesses and the businesses that are struggling has much more to do with ignorance, confusion, and inattention to most of these seven main parts than how great the products or services are that the business produces.

RJon's business, How to Manage Enterprises, helps hundreds of—perhaps, by the time you read this, more than a thousand—small business owners manage and keep each of the *seven main parts of a successful business* in alignment. But this book is focused on the foundational first of those parts of a successful business: marketing—and we touch upon sales a bit too. That's because if your marketing does its job well, then sales is simplified and more efficient, which is an important detail to keep in mind. But too many entrepreneurs confuse the two concepts.

So here it is:

Marketing is everything that happens to get the right customers with the right needs and the right expectations to your business. They should arrive already prequalified, preeducated, preconditioned, and therefore predisposed to do business with you when they arrive.

Many entrepreneurs are surprised to know that part of the job of marketing is also to screen out the wrong kind of prospects—or even the right kind of prospects with the wrong needs and expectations—and protect the business's resources from being consumed by them.

And more than a few struggling entrepreneurs have been upset at the notion that part of the job of marketing is also to regulate the flow of prospects coming in at the top of the funnel in order to protect their reputation and cash flow by not overwhelming production capacity. If a person is dying of thirst in a desert, it's understandable that the notion of having too much of a good thing might be foreign to him or her.

An Automatic Marketing Machine allows you to align the flow of new prospects with your business's capacity to serve them all … which is part of the secret of how we maximize the lifetime value of our relationship with each customer, turning one into two and so many more.

Sales (when done the right way) is an ethical, professional, predictable, and highly profitable system for helping prospects think through and get clarity about where they are today with their situation versus where they would prefer to be tomorrow versus where they would like to avoid being tomorrow if they don't get some help.

Unfortunately, many prospects walk into a place of business with important problems and walk back out with the same important problems still unresolved. This is because most entrepreneurs have never been trained how to professionally and ethically sell their products and services.

Most entrepreneurs don't understand what you now *do* understand about the role of marketing in their business … and so they rely too heavily on sales instead of creating an Automatic Marketing Machine and letting it do its job.

DON'T BE AFRAID TO ROCK THE BOAT

By now it's becoming clear that building an Automatic Marketing Machine for your business is going to push you outside of your comfort zone. We're going to ask you to think about things differently and to *do* things differently than just about every other business owner in your town.

Be prepared for skepticism and criticism. Your peers might think you're crazy. They won't like your advertisements. They will probably start talking about you behind your back.

When that starts to happen, remember that most of your peers are struggling or on the verge of failure. They are operating businesses that do not have a marketing machine in place, and so they're likely stressed about cash flow, about making payroll, about paying their bills each month.

Given that backdrop, you should consider it a good thing that your marketing strategy is dramatically different from those of your peers! Don't be afraid to rock the boat.

CHAPTER FIVE

TEN FOUNDATIONAL RULES TO BUILD YOUR AUTOMATIC MARKETING MACHINE

E very profitable marketing machine follows certain rules. These are not rules we just made up. They're rules we've observed over and over again in some of the most effective marketing machines we've worked on and studied. When you follow these rules, your marketing machine is going to be a *lot* more likely to work than when you break them.

Look, we're not saying no one has ever built a profitable, predictable, reliable, and cost-effective marketing machine that breaks these rules. There are obviously exceptions to every rule. And if you want to waste the next ten years of your life experimenting instead of making a profit … then go ahead and figure out how to build an

Automatic Marketing Machine with a different set of rules, and then let us know where we can buy your book to learn how you did it!

In the meantime we're going to keep making millions of dollars for ourselves and hundreds of millions of dollars for our clients by sticking with these simple and proven-to-work rules for building and maintaining an Automatic Marketing Machine.

Yes, we know this sounds kind of pompous—but we're just trying to make a point. We're both really sick of seeing entrepreneurs like you, people who have so much value to give the world with your innovative products and services that really do make your customers' lives better when they finally find and choose to do business with you … we are just so sick and tired of watching entrepreneurs starve while they screw around, trying to reinvent the wheel. And if you want to know what *really* pisses us off, it's those marketers who make things up and overcomplicate the marketing of a small business just to sell the new latest, greatest marketing idea that's so brand new and amazingly innovative that no one has even had any time to put it to the test in the real world to prove that it works.

Like we said, our goal is to help you build a marketing machine that works. We're not here to impress you with a bunch of new ideas that sound good in theory but haven't been around long enough to be put to the test.

Recall from the introduction of this book that we are *not* claiming we invented a whole new science of marketing. If you're already an experienced marketer, there's probably not much in this book you haven't heard about before. Instead, what this book is meant to do is lay out for the small business owners who don't aspire to become marketing gurus a simple, proven, cost-effective, and reliable marketing machine that brings you high-quality leads automatically day in and day out for years to come.

So can we just agree that you'll follow these rules we're about to lay out for you and give them a chance to work for you before you start trying to get creative?

These rules should be used to govern every single marketing campaign, every advertisement, every marketing tactic. Your marketing vendors must adhere to these rules in all the marketing they manage for you.

These rules will serve as guardrails while you develop your marketing machine. They will keep you on course and prevent you from making the mistakes that most small businesses make with their marketing.

They will force your marketing vendors to operate with transparency so that you can hold them accountable for the results they produce.

If you follow these rules, you will have visibility into your marketing campaigns—allowing you to see what's working and what's not working and allowing you to change course quickly when necessary.

By the way, you can scan the QR code below or visit www.AutomaticMarketingMachine.com/10Rules for a printable version of these foundational rules that you can download, print, and put on your wall. And tell your marketing vendor to do the same!

Rule #1: Every Advertisement Will Include a Call to Action

Every social media ad. Every landing page. Every magazine ad. Every single advertisement you produce must contain a clear, specific, measurable call to action (CTA) asking its audience to take your desired next step.

- "Click here to download the free resource."

- "Fill out the form to register for the webinar."

- "Call now to request your free consultation."

- "Subscribe to the newsletter for more free content."

- "RSVP for the lunch-and-learn to save your seat."

This discipline is what distinguishes direct response marketing (which is the philosophy your Automatic Marketing Machine is built on) from brand-based marketing (which will burn through your marketing budget and leave you penniless).

Every single advertisement you produce must contain a clear, specific, measurable call to action.

This discipline allows you to create accountability, and it allows you to easily diagnose each component of your marketing machine. If every single advertisement, every landing page, every piece of marketing collateral has a measurable call to action … then you have the ability to assess performance with a simple yes-or-no question. Are your prospects taking the desired action in response to the advertisement?

Once you start thinking this way, you'll begin to identify new places to include your CTAs. For example, you could include a QR code on your business card with a CTA offering a free special resource for download. You can include CTAs when you give presentations. You can include CTAs in your office signage. You can even include a CTA in your email signature—and when you consider how many emails you and your team send each day, it will probably start to feel like criminal negligence if you *don't* include a CTA in your email signature.

If you'd like some CTA ideas for your own email signature, scan the QR code below or visit www.AutomaticMarketingMachine.com/CTA for a handful of high-performing CTAs that you can swipe and deploy immediately!

(Do you see what we just did?)

Rule #2: You Will Create Urgency

The purpose of every advertisement is to elicit a response from its audience. And *urgency* is the critical ingredient that must be present in order to drive action. If you don't give your audience a good reason to take action *right now*, then it doesn't matter how attractive and well-thought-out your advertisement is—they may like it, find it compelling, find it interesting, find it persuasive … but they're not going to *do* anything about it.

Why?

Because they're *busy*. They're distracted. They've *already* got a long to-do list, and as much as they may be interested in what you have to say, they're not going to take action unless you present them with a compelling reason to do so.

Which is why you *must* create urgency in every single advertisement.

Rule #3: You Will Make It *Easy* to Respond

Even if you've followed the first two rules to a *T*—you've clearly identified your CTA, and you've created a compelling reason to take action *now*—you will lose many potential prospects if you make it too difficult for them to respond.

The fewer hoops you ask them to jump through, the better your response rate is going to be.

There are a few things to keep in mind.

First, your instructions have to be clear and simple. Do *not* ask your prospects to think too hard, or you *will* lose them. Don't send them off on a wild goose chase.

Instead, roll out the metaphorical red carpet and make it incredibly obvious what they're supposed to do next. That's why, for example, it's important to use dedicated landing pages to make your offer rather than sending them to your website home page.

On the home page, they'll have too many options and be liable to get confused and distracted and to wander off the path you've asked them to take.

Second, don't ask them to jump through any more hoops than absolutely necessary. If you're asking them to register for a webinar, don't ask them for any more information than you need.

You'll want to capture their name and email address, and you may need to ask for their phone number, but you probably don't need to get their mailing address, and you definitely don't need to ask them for their Social Security number.

The more you ask of your prospects, the less likely they are to comply. So you need to be strategic and ask only for the information that you absolutely need.

Third, the actual layout and functionality of your landing pages, registration forms, order forms, and other response mechanisms are very important. If you're running a digital campaign, remember that a sizable percentage—often a majority—of your prospects will encounter your advertising on a mobile device. And so your ads, forms, and landing pages must be optimized for mobile screens.

Want more help creating landing pages that really work? Scan the QR code or visit www.AutomaticMarketing Machine.com/LandingPage for a short video lesson that walks you through the basics!

This concept is important off-line too. If you're asking prospects to call your office and schedule a consultation, you'd best be sure that whoever answers the phone is going to be friendly, competent, and ready to assist.

As you're planning your marketing campaigns and building your marketing machine, operate with the assumption that your prospects are busy, distractible, easily confused, and easily discouraged.

Design your campaigns so that even the least competent, least tech-savvy, most easily defeated individuals will *still* be able to respond to your CTA and follow your instructions.

Make it *easy*.

Rule #4: You Will Use Strong Copy

A pretty picture or an attractive graphic may catch someone's attention—but it takes persuasive *language* to drive action. Too many business owners make the fatal mistake of delegating their marketing campaigns to *graphic designers*.

Say it with us, please: graphic design does not equal marketing.

Graphic design plays an important role in most marketing campaigns, and graphic designers are an essential part of your marketing team—make no mistake about that. But ultimately, graphic design exists to facilitate, support, and enhance the message that is delivered with *words*.

Which means that your advertisements must include strong, persuasive copy if you are going to be successful.

Effective marketing copy is written in language that resonates with the target audience.

Effective marketing copy speaks directly to the pain points that its target audience is experiencing.

Effective marketing copy paints a picture of a brighter future once the pain point has been resolved.

Effective marketing copy presents a binary choice to the audience—either they are *in*, or they are out in the cold.

Strong, persuasive copy is a necessary ingredient of any successful advertisement or marketing campaign.

Rule #5: You Will Create Automated, Organized Follow-Up Systems

Follow-up is the secret ingredient that powers all successful marketing campaigns. And strong, organized, automated follow-up is a critical component of your Automatic Marketing Machine.

Follow-up is necessary at virtually every step of a marketing campaign. For example, let's say you're running a very simple social media campaign that goes something like this:

Step one: An advertisement runs on Facebook promoting a piece of downloadable content—let's call it a special report.

Step two: Once the prospect clicks on the ad, they are taken to a landing page where they can download the report by completing your sign-up form.

Step three: Once the prospect downloads the report, you send them a call to action inviting them to schedule an appointment with your team.

Step four: Once the prospect schedules this meeting, they receive an email confirming their appointment and sharing important logistic details, such as driving directions.

What you have to understand is that every single step in this very simple campaign requires multiple follow-up communications in order to keep the prospect on track.

The Facebook ad in step one probably has to be shown at least ten times before the prospect will respond.

Then, once they've visited the landing page, they will usually have to be retargeted several times before they actually complete it.

Once they've downloaded the report, they'll usually need a minimum of three follow-up emails before they schedule a consultation.

And once they've scheduled their consultation, they'll need an entirely new sequence of follow-up emails to make sure they show up on time, in the right place, and in the right state of mind.

So you see, even a simple four-step campaign likely requires twenty or more follow-up communications for each prospect that it generates.

And that's just one campaign. You also need to have systems in place to ensure that you're following up with past customers and clients, encouraging them to hire you again or to refer their friends and family to you.

You need systems in place to follow up with your referral network—frequent touchpoints to maintain top-of-mind awareness and remind them what a good referral opportunity looks like.

You need follow-up systems for lost prospects who have not yet engaged your business.

If this sounds overwhelming, don't worry. Remember, we're building an *Automatic* Marketing Machine for your business, which means that once you build it, you don't have to lift a finger … it just runs, and runs, and runs.

Meanwhile, most small business marketing fails in large part because business owners don't have follow-up systems in place. It's truly a shame because they've already done so much of the work. They've created the ads; they've built the landing pages. They might even be capturing leads through their landing pages.

But because they don't have strong follow-up systems in place, most of their potential leads will never come to fruition.

Their loss. Your gain.

Rule #6: There Will Be a Measurable Objective Behind Every Campaign

There is an epidemic of wasteful marketing, and countless small businesses fall prey. Huge sums of money are wasted, month after month after month, on marketing that fails to produce results.

Now, let's be clear about something: failed marketing campaigns are inevitable. Even the best, most accomplished, most well-resourced marketing professionals in the world regularly experience failure.

That's because marketing isn't an exact science. Marketing requires engaging with human beings, which means that logic and reason may or may not work. Any given marketing campaign is also subject to the environmental conditions around it—the state of the economy, what happened in the latest news cycle, even the weather.

So, for a variety of reasons, **failed campaigns are inevitable.** So the key to success isn't *avoiding failure,* because that's impossible. <u>The key to success is identifying failure so that you stop wasting resources and pivot in another direction.</u>

And the key to identifying failure is determining, ahead of time, how you will judge a marketing campaign's success. And then by committing to reviewing on a regular basis performance against the objective indicators you've selected.

Note the word *objective.* Remember, you can't judge a marketing campaign using intangible criteria. How it makes you feel, how it looks, what your friends and family say, what your colleagues think— none of this is objective data, and none of this should be used to define success.

Objective indicators are quantitative. How much did you spend on your campaign? And with that spend, how many prospects did you reach with your ads? How many responded to your ad by visiting your landing page? How many people who reached your landing page completed the form? How many of those people scheduled a consultation? How many of those people showed up for their consultation? And how many of those people become paying customers of your business?

So before you launch a campaign, get clear about the metrics that will indicate success or failure. And then develop the discipline of regularly *reviewing* performance of the campaign against the metrics that you've identified.

Developing this habit will not make you immune to failed campaigns. But it will enable you to quickly identify failed campaigns and divert your resources into campaigns that are performing better. This is the difference between the long-term success or failure of your marketing machine!

Remember, you can visit www.AutomaticMarketing Machine.com/KPIs to download a simple, customizable template that you can use to track your marketing KPIs and hold your vendors accountable! Or just scan the QR code below:

Rule #7: There Will Be Split Testing

Big doors swing on small hinges. And the difference between the success or failure of any given ad, email blast, or landing page can be surprisingly small.

We have a lot of personal experience and evidence to back this point up!

Over the last twelve years, we've managed hundreds of marketing campaigns involving *thousands* of ads and landing pages.

And we have consistently observed that very small details make a huge difference in the performance of each piece of the campaign—the individual ads, landing pages, and follow-up sequences.

For example, we once saw a landing page conversion rate increase from 13 percent to 21 percent when we changed the color of the submit button from yellow to red. That's it—that was the only change.

The content remained the same. The layout remained the same. The offer was the same. All that changed was the color of the button, and conversion rate increased by 8 percent.

Which meant that our cost per lead decreased significantly, and the campaign was much more profitable. All because we changed the color of the button!

So now you can probably guess why it's very important to split test your marketing campaigns. Split testing just means testing different versions of the ad or landing page in order to determine which version performs best.

For example, you can test things like …

- your ad headline

- ad copy

- ad layout

- ad images/video
- landing page headlines
- landing page content
- landing page length
- landing page colors
- landing page button placement

Split testing can make a huge difference in campaign performance. Sometimes it results in modest improvements. Other times it's the difference between earning a negative ROI and a positive ROI on the campaign. Still other times it takes a campaign from moderately profitable to spectacularly profitable.

Split testing is a nonnegotiable step in building out your Automatic Marketing Machine!

Yet most businesses never bother to split test their marketing campaigns. And they leave money on the table every time they fail to do this.

Split testing is a nonnegotiable step in building out your Automatic Marketing Machine!

Rule #8: There Will Be Measurement and Accountability

Every campaign must have predetermined, quantifiable, objective measures of success. And—this is critical—you must develop the discipline to review this data on a regular basis.

Repeat: You *must* develop the discipline to *review* your campaign KPIs on a regular cadence.

Not only will you *review* the data, but you will make informed decisions based on the data. If a campaign is falling short of its objectives, as evidenced by the data you're reviewing, you have a few options:

1. **Give it more time**. If you've just launched the campaign, or if your budget is low, you may simply need to give it time in order to collect more data.

2. **Make a change**. If the campaign isn't performing up to your expectations, you may need to shake things up. Try new ads. Try new language on the landing page. Try a different offer. And see if performance turns around.

3. **Pull the plug.** If the campaign isn't performing, and you've gathered enough data to feel confident in your assessment, and there are no further changes likely to turn performance around—it's time to pull the plug.

Remember—*pulling the plug isn't a bad outcome!* Of course we'd all prefer every campaign to be successful, but failure is inevitable—and you scored a huge win because you were able to spot the failed campaign and cut your losses.

Make sure you scan the QR code or visit www.automatic marketingmachine.com/KPIs in order to download a simple template you can use to track campaign data.

There's a popular quote from the legendary nineteenth-century retailer John Wanamaker that goes something like this:

"Half my advertising spend is wasted; the trouble is, I don't know which half."

That may have been true in Wanamaker's day, but there's no excuse for letting that become a reality in your business today.

The philosophy of direct response marketing combined with the sophisticated tracking and measurement tools we have available today mean that there is simply no reason you can't demand measurement and hold your marketing vendors accountable for performance.

There *will* be measurement and accountability. Accept nothing less.

Rule #9: You Will Not Be Swayed by Opinion—Only Facts

A sure sign of an amateur marketer is that they spend a *lot* of time debating matters of preference.

"I think it looks better in blue."

"I think it sounds better *this* way."

"I think we should use *this* graphic instead."

The right way to make these types of decisions is by testing, measuring, and then making a data-based decision.

Some of the highest-performing marketing campaigns either of us have ever run have been *ugly*! Ugly ads, ugly landing pages.

And if we had just let our *subjective* preferences dictate, we would have replaced them with something prettier—but because we track and measure data, we were able to determine that the ugly landing page was actually outperforming the "prettier" pages we split tested against.

Be very, very careful not to let feelings or preferences dictate your marketing decision-making process.

When someone on your marketing team asks you, "Do you think we should do it *this way*, or should we try it *this way instead?*" your response should generally be, "Let's test them both and see what works better!"

Your team's opinion doesn't matter. Your own opinion doesn't matter. The opinions of your friends, your family, and your colleagues definitely don't matter. The only opinions that matter are those of your audiences, and they indicate their decisions through their trackable, measurable actions.

Opinions don't matter. Personal preferences don't matter. Performance matters. Stick to the facts, and make sure your team does too.

Rule #10: Results Matter; Everything Else Is Window Dressing

The purpose of your marketing is to generate qualified prospects for your business.

That's it.

The purpose of your marketing is *not* to look pretty, or massage your ego, or impress your parents.

Every dollar, every resource, every minute of time that you invest into your marketing is done with the purpose of generating qualified prospects for your business.

If a given ad, landing page, campaign, or initiative isn't producing results … stop doing it.

Stick to this mantra, and you will save yourself tens of thousands of dollars in wasted marketing spend, countless hours of wasted time, and endless frustration.

Check your ego at the door. Leave your opinions at home. Results rule … period.

CHAPTER SIX

AIMING YOUR MACHINE

The first step in designing a machine—any machine, from a water pump to a printing press to the space shuttle—is to clearly define the purpose for which you are creating the machine.

What problem is the machine intended to solve? And how will you know whether or not the machine is successful?

- The water pump is designed to move water from point A to point B.

- The printing press is designed to quickly and accurately print books, letters, and documents.

- The space shuttle is designed to take humans to space and to keep them safe during their journey.

A clear aim. And a clear definition of success. This information serves to keep the designers of the machine focused on the right objectives, and it provides the operators of the machine with a framework against which they can measure performance of the machine.

So let's be clear: *the purpose of your Automatic Marketing Machine is to generate a steady supply of qualified prospects for your business.*

That's the mission. And that's how we'll gauge the success of your marketing machine.

You should know that this is not an arbitrary objective. It has been carefully chosen. The coauthors of this book have collectively worked with tens of thousands of small business owners and have a deep understanding of the intricacies of building a successful business.

This is why we can tell (and keep telling) you with so much certainty that without a steady supply of new prospects whom you can reliably convert into paying customers and ideally cause to become referral sources, too, nothing else matters.

Your professional credentials don't matter. Your reputation in the community doesn't matter. Your past performance doesn't matter. Your work ethic doesn't matter. Your website doesn't matter. The quality of your products and services doesn't matter.

Without a steady, predictable stream of new prospects into your business, nothing else really matters. And frankly, life becomes very difficult.

If you don't have a steady stream of new prospects, you will feel compelled to accept every customer who walks in the door. You will hate yourself for doing it, but eventually the very real prospect of going out of business will cause you to talk yourself into taking on work that you don't like doing for customers whom you don't like working with.

Because you don't have a steady stream of new prospects, you can't afford to build your team.

You're stuck doing most of the work yourself, which keeps you in the business all day, every day, including evenings and a lot of weekends.

Because you don't have a steady stream of new prospects, you can't afford the office space you'd really like to have. You can't afford the technology you know you need to serve your customers at the highest possible level.

Because you don't have a steady stream of new prospects, you're stressed out about cash flow.

You're worried about meeting payroll.

You're dreading the moment when you have to tell your spouse, again, that there's not enough profit left over at the end of the month to pay yourself for the blood, sweat, and tears you've poured into the firm.

Everything Changes When You Build an Automatic Marketing Machine

Now imagine a world in which you wake up in the morning, refreshed after a good night's sleep, with no anxiety about your cash flow. No stress about making payroll on Friday. No concern about when, where, and how the next prospect will show up to your business.

Imagine a world in which you wake up every morning knowing what your income will be for the next three months, the next six months, the next twelve months, the next eighteen months.

Imagine waking up in the morning knowing where your next five, ten, twenty, fifty prospects are going to come from and knowing approximately when they'll arrive. Imagine waking up and enjoying a slow, *relaxing* morning because you have a marketing machine in place that is consistently, predictably, reliably generating a steady stream of new customers for your business.

Imagine going on a long vacation and then returning to your office to find that your business actually *grew* in your absence ... because you have a marketing machine that works for you, automatically, whether you're in the office or in court or lying on the beach.

This isn't a fantasy—it's reality for hundreds and hundreds of small businesses just like yours all across the country. It's reality for businesses in every industry you can think of, in big cities and small towns, built by men and built by women, right handed and left handed ... and it can work for you too.

Get out your notebook and your calendar—because we're about to roll up our sleeves and get to work.

CHAPTER SEVEN

GLOSSARY OF IMPORTANT TERMS AND KEY CONCEPTS

T his is a strange place for a glossary!

But we have found that our team gets dramatically better results with our clients when we begin by educating them about some key terms. It's always disappointing to us whenever we get a new client who comes to us from a big fancy marketing agency and they've been kept in the dark. They're just completely ignorant of what these key terms mean. I mean, how are you supposed to have a productive conversation with your marketing vendor if you don't speak the language? That's a rhetorical question, obviously. We'll leave it to you to decide for yourself why a marketing agency might not want their client to feel empowered to speak their language.

We're about to change gears. The whole first part of the book is meant to open your mind to a whole new way of thinking about the marketing of your business. If you've made it this far, you should now find yourself thinking very differently about the marketing of not only your business ... you should find yourself thinking very differently about all the marketing you see all around you!

Every time you drive by a billboard at the side of the road and there's no call to action, no way to track results.

Every time you open a magazine and see a big beautiful picture of a celebrity next to a clever slogan but no call to action, no way to track results.

Every time you see it happening, you'll know you're witnessing another marketing victim.

Every time you see a commercial and you don't see any way for the business owner who is paying for it to measure ROI by message or by the time of day an ad runs or even by the station.

Every time you opt in for something and the business owner who worked so hard and paid so much to get you to opt in for their free report or their free course or whatever it is they used to get you to raise your hand and announce, "I'm a hot prospect! I deserve special attention! You really should be investing most of your marketing budget to get me over the goal line because I'm right here at the edge and just really busy and distracted and it's not my job to remember to buy your products or services" ... and then no one follows up with you.

Every time you see it happening right before your very eyes or you experience it yourself as a consumer, you'll know you're witnessing another marketing victim. Another bucket hauler being asked (or forced) to carry their own water from a river somewhere to keep their business alive while their marketing vendors sell them leaky buckets!

Now we are shifting gears from foundational theory to practical application. And so it's important that we're all on the same page with our terminology. The following are some of the most common technical terms that will come up when you're having a marketing conversation with someone who knows what they're talking about:

A/B testing: This refers to the process of testing two marketing assets against each other to see which performs best. For example, testing two different images as part of a display ad allows you to determine which generates a better response. Also referred to as split testing.

Analytics: Data related to the performance of a website, ad campaign, funnel, email campaign, etc. Analytics allow you to monitor performance of your various marketing assets and campaigns.

Bounce rate: The percentage of visitors to a landing page or website that bounce—which means they quickly leave the page without engaging. The lower the bounce rate, the better your page is performing.

Call to action: The part of your advertisement, landing page, or campaign that asks your audience to take a specific action. For example, "Call (XXX) XXX-XXXX to schedule a free introductory session" is a call to action. Often abbreviated as CTA.

Clicks: When a prospect literally clicks on a button or a link in your advertisement, which typically drives them to a landing page or some type of offer.

Click-through rate: The number of people who click on your advertisement divided by the number of people who were exposed to your advertisement. If your ad was shown to 1,000 people and 50 people clicked on it, 50 divided by 1,000 gives you a 5 percent click-through rate. Often abbreviated as CTR.

Customer avatar: A detailed description of your target customer. A customer avatar includes both demographic and psychographic information about your target customer.

Conversion rate: The number of people who convert on your landing page or website, typically by filling out a form or calling your phone number, divided by the total number of visitors to your landing page or website. If 1,000 people visit your landing page and 75 of them fill out your form, 75 divided by 1,000 gives you a 7.5 percent conversion rate.

Content marketing: Developing content—such as blog entries, articles, videos, white papers, e-books, and special reports—in order to attract prospects to your business.

Cost of acquisition: The average cost to generate a new customer. For example, if you spend $5,000 on a Google Ads campaign and generate ten clients as a result, your cost of acquisition is $500. Often abbreviated as CoA.

Drip campaign: A multistep follow-up campaign (often email based) that takes place over a period of weeks, months, or even years. In a typical drip campaign, prospects are emailed several times per month until they eventually convert to paying customers.

Pay-per-click ads: Ads in which your business is charged only when somebody clicks on the ad. Distinct from other forms of advertising that charge you per impression or for the duration of time that your ad is displayed.

Impressions: The number of times your ad has been viewed in a given time period. Note that one person could see the ad multiple times, and each viewing would be an impression. If you see an ad three times in one day, you would have received three impressions.

Funnel: A multistep marketing campaign in which you ask your prospects to take several steps in their journey toward becoming customers. For example, step one in the funnel may be downloading a white paper. Step two may be attending a webinar. Step three could be finally scheduling their appointment.

Key Performance Indicator: Key metrics that reveal whether or not a campaign is performing according to your expectations. For example, landing page conversion rate is a common key performance indicator in a lead generation campaign. Often abbreviated as KPI.

Reach: The number of *unique* individuals you've reached with an advertising campaign. Multiple impressions from the same individual don't change your reach. For example, if the same person sees your ad three times, you've created three impressions, but your reach is one.

Search Engine Optimization: The process of optimizing a website so that it appears closer to the top of search engine results. Note that search engine optimization impacts organic (unpaid) search listings, not paid listings. Often abbreviated as SEO.

Paid search: A type of ad campaign in which you pay a search engine—such as Google or Yahoo!—to display your ads when certain key phrases are searched for.

Landing page: A web page focused on a specific offer or outcome. The objective of a landing page is to drive visitors to take a specific action—such as downloading a white paper or scheduling an appointment. A landing page, unlike a normal website page, does not provide a navigation menu because the goal is to keep the visitor on the landing page until they take action.

Lead: A prospect who has raised their hand and indicated that they are interested in your services. Sometimes they do this by calling your business to schedule an appointment. Other times they download a white paper or attend a webinar. There are many ways that someone can become a lead for your business, and we discuss this in depth in chapter 9.

Lead magnet: A free report, white paper, video series, or some other type of free content that you give away to your prospects in exchange for their contact information so that you can follow up with them later.

Qualified lead: A lead that meets objective criteria that makes them a good candidate for your services. For example, a married man, with children, between the ages of thirty-five and fifty-five who lives in your town and is planning to get divorced could be a qualified lead for a family law firm.

Unqualified lead: A lead that *does not* meet objective criteria and therefore is not a good candidate for your services, despite the fact that they reached out to your business for help.

Organic social media: Content posted on your social media profiles without an advertising spend attached to it.

Paid social media: Content posted on social media and then promoted to a much wider distribution through a paid advertising campaign.

If you're reading this book, we encourage you to fold down the first page of this chapter to make it easy for you to refer to as we move into the practical-application sections of this book. And if you're listening to the audio version of this book, you can scan visit www.AutomaticMarketingMachine.com/Vocabulary to download a PDF you can print out and keep at the ready the next time you're trying to have an intelligent conversation with any of your marketing vendors to get a straight answer to the most important question you should hope they're losing sleep over to keep earning your business: "Is it working?"

CHAPTER EIGHT

MARKET, MESSAGE, MEDIA

I t's time to get down to business. Let's talk about *how* to begin building your Automatic Marketing Machine.

There are a couple of things to keep in mind before we get started:

First, remember—especially if you're brand new to marketing—that it's OK to take things slowly as you get started.

Villages don't transition from the bucket system of manually gathering water to fully automatic indoor plumbing overnight. It's an incremental process, and it starts with creating simple contraptions like wells, water catchment tanks, and pipes before eventually developing modern plumbing. Plus the villagers have to adapt themselves to a new way of living. All that time that gets freed up needs to be intentionally redeployed, or else there's a real risk of backsliding … because when you're used to spending the majority of your waking hours hauling buckets back and forth from the river, and all of a sudden you don't have to do it anymore … what *are* you supposed to do with your time?

Yeah, of course you should probably start planting crops or start a business ... but when you have spent your entire life hauling water buckets back and forth to the river ... you haven't exactly had time to learn how to manage crops or build a business.

It takes time to adapt to this new way of living, and if it all happens too quickly, it could blow up in your face.

In fact, do you want to know the number one reason we get from clients for why they discontinue our services and sabotage their Automatic Marketing Machine? It's because it all works too well, and the rest of their business—and in fact the rest of their whole life—isn't equipped for this much growth!

So don't worry if your first steps in building your Automatic Marketing Machine are simple and even primitive compared to businesses that have been doing this for a long time. And don't judge your beginning by someone else's middle or end! Instead just focus on making progress. Our best clients are people who have the entrepreneurial maturity to let us help them take small steps every month, and then all of the sudden they wake up in ten or twelve months with a completely new and better business and life, and they get to join our Overnight Success Club.

Seriously, if you could double your business in twelve months, you really *would* look like an overnight success to most other business owners. In fact they'd probably call it a miracle. So take a breath, count to ten, and let's just focus on taking the first steps. There will be *plenty* of time to test, refine, improve, and scale as we go.

Second, please keep in mind that none of your marketing machinery needs to be particularly complicated—it should actually be pretty simple and easy to understand!

By the way—anytime you are having a conversation with a marketing vendor and they start using fancy terminology that doesn't make sense to you, it should trigger a red flag. Ask them to start again and explain themselves in plain English.

More often than not, when a marketing vendor is making something sound complicated, it's because they're trying to hide something or distract you from something. Or else maybe they themselves don't understand it well enough to explain it in simple terms. Truly, there is absolutely nothing about any of this stuff that any reasonably intelligent twelve-year-old shouldn't be able to understand and explain to another reasonably intelligent twelve-year-old.

Seriously, if a concept or idea doesn't make sense to you and the person who is spending your marketing dollars can't explain it in a way that *does* make sense to you, put down the bucket they sold you, because there's a good chance there's a big hole in it!

There are really just three simple variables that go into any marketing or advertising campaign, and that's what this chapter is all about:

Market. Message. Media.

Market refers to your target audience. This is the *who* in your marketing campaign—as in, Who are you targeting? The more specifically you can define your target market, the more precisely your marketing machine can be calibrated, and the more effective it will become.

Message refers to the language and the offer in your campaign. What are you offering, and what language are you using in order to persuade your target audience to take action?

Media is simply how your message is delivered to your market. What channel(s) are you using? Keep in mind that media does not necessarily refer to mass media. Your media could be social media advertisements or TV commercials—but it could also be networking and face-to-face conversations. How are you getting your message in front of your target market and ideally no one else?

If your marketing campaigns are going to work, you have to get all three of these elements right. Two out of three isn't good enough.

- A campaign with a brilliant message and the perfect media strategy won't generate results if you target the wrong audience.

- Or you might have your target audience dialed in, and you might have a great message figured out, but if you can't get your great message in front of your well-defined target audience, it's not going to work.

- And without a compelling message, it doesn't matter that you've identified the right target market and figured out a media channel that allows you to reach them. The whole thing falls apart if you don't have a persuasive message that drives your audience to take action.

Market. Message. Media.

You have to get all three right.

MARKET: FIND YOUR STARVING CROWD

Gary Halbert, known as one of the best and most successful direct response copywriters of all time, used to ask his students the following question:

"If you were starting a hamburger stand on the beach and could choose one 'advantage' to have on your side during this venture, what would it be?"

His students would often choose advantages like high-quality ingredients, friendly waitstaff, low prices, an ideal location, or really large signage.

Gary would respond that there is *one* advantage that is more important than everything else combined. An advantage that would absolutely guarantee success.

That advantage: A *starving crowd.*

It's pretty easy to sell a lot of hamburgers when you're surrounded by really hungry customers!

A SIMPLE EXERCISE TO IDENTIFY YOUR TARGET MARKET

Here's a fun exercise to help you get crystal clear on who your ideal prospects are. Put this book down, grab a notepad, and make a list of your top ten favorite customers that you've worked with over the years. These are the customers who you'd love to duplicate over and over again!

Once you've got your list of ten customers, think through what traits they have in common.

Start with their demographics:

- What's their gender?

- How old are they?

- What's their relationship status?

- How many kids do they have?

- What ages are their kids?

- Where do they live?

- Do they own a home? How much is it worth?

- What type of job do they have?

- What language do they speak?

- What type of car do they drive?

Then do their psychographics as well:

- What values are important to them?

- What type of media do they consume?

- What do they do for fun?

- Are they religious?

- How do they view the world?

- Who are they angry with, and why?

- What are their hopes and dreams and aspirations? And why?

As you complete this exercise for all ten of your favorite customers, look for the trends.

What are the common characteristics that your best customers have in common? Do you think that's just a coincidence? Try expanding the list to your top twenty, your top one hundred. And what if it is just a coincidence? At this point a lot of would-be, potentially successful entrepreneurs are going to go down the very unprofitable rabbit hole of trying to figure out *why* their best customers or clients or patients or passengers all have in common what you're going to find your best customers have in common.

Who cares? OK, if you *really* want to figure this out, do this: follow the instructions in this book and in the bonus materials to build a kick-ass Automatic Marketing Machine. Then visit www. AutomaticMarketingMachine.com/Contest to enter our annual contest for the best Automatic Marketing Machine, and if your entry places in the top ten, we'll invite you to a very special and totally pointless workshop entitled "Let's Look Our Gift Horse in the Mouth." This is a very expensive workshop we run every year for some very successful marketers whose Automatic Marketing Machines are working so well that they have a ton of extra disposable income and plenty of free time on their hands to sit around in exotic places with us and hypothesize why the things that are working so well are working so well.

Now, make a second list on your notepad. But this time, list your top ten *least favorite* customers of all time. Customers that you'd prefer not to ever do business with again.

When you're done, you'll not only have a clear picture of the types of prospects you want to attract into your business—you'll also have a clear picture of the types of prospects we want to calibrate your Automatic Marketing Machine to protect you and your staff from.

Think of this as calibrating your marketing machine—because the whole point of building your Automatic Marketing Machine is to attract the type of prospects that you want to engage your business and to keep everyone else away!

Want to make this even easier? Visit www.AutomaticMarketing Machine.com/avatar and download the *free* target market profile worksheet we've created to help you through this important exercise. Or scan the QR code below:

CRAFT A MESSAGE THAT'S IRRESISTIBLE TO YOUR TARGET CUSTOMERS

Now that you've got a clear picture of *who* you want to attract to your business, it's time to start working on your messaging.

The first thing to understand is that nobody wakes up in the morning thinking about you and your business. They're thinking about themselves and their life. They're thinking about everything they've got to do that day. They're thinking about what they're going to have for breakfast. They're thinking about their family.

They're definitely *not* thinking about you and your business. They might, however, be facing some significant challenges or problems in their life. Or they might be thinking about some significant opportunities in their life.

The first thing to understand is that nobody wakes up in the morning thinking about you and your business.

The key to effective messaging, then, is helping your ideal prospects understand how your products and services can solve their problems and/ or take advantage of opportunities so that they—your customers—can improve their lives and have a better future.

That is what your customers are interested in—how to have a better future for themselves and the people they care about.

Your business and your products and services ... are simply the means to their end.

Don't get offended! We promised you the truth, right? Not a bunch of BS to make you feel great about yourself.

So let's recognize that this is simply how human beings are wired.

We're primarily self-interested. Each of us is the hero of our own story. Your job, if you want your business to sell millions and millions of dollars' worth of products and services, is to help the hero understand how engaging your business will create a better future.

Most small businesses never figure this out. And that's one major reason why their marketing doesn't work very well.

Most marketing is focused on how great the *business* is, not on how they're going to make life better for their prospects and customers.

THINGS YOUR CUSTOMERS DON'T CARE ABOUT:

- What school you attended
- The awards you've earned
- How long you've been in business
- How large or small your staff is
- How hard you work every day
- The nitty-gritty details—a.k.a. how the sausage gets made

THINGS YOUR CUSTOMERS DO CARE ABOUT:

- Creating a brighter future for themselves and the people they love

Now, here's the thing. In order to create really good, truly powerful messaging, we can't *guess* at what motivates our prospects. We need to know—for certain—what really motivates them. What really keeps them up at night. What they're really trying to accomplish in their lives. What they really want their futures to look like.

So—get those pens out again—it's time for another exercise.

Step one: Find the list of your top ten favorite customers that you made earlier in this chapter.

Step two: Pull your notepad out and put yourself in their shoes as best you can. The goal here is to really, truly, deeply understand their mindset and their motivations so that you can develop messaging that actually resonates. Answer these questions:

- What keeps them lying awake at night, mind racing and stomach churning, unable to sleep?

- What are they talking to their spouse about, obsessively, angrily, when they're driving home from the restaurant? What are they angry about? Who are they angry with? And why?

- Even if they won't admit it to anyone else ... What are they afraid of? What terrifies them? What creates visceral knots in their stomach every time they think about it? What are they afraid of happening ... or not happening?

- What are their daily frustrations and pet peeves?

Now ask them to think about the moment they first contacted your business:

- What was the specific problem (or opportunity) that motivated them to do business with your company?

- What problems were being created in their life because of this problem? And how did those problems make them feel?

- How different will their life look once they address the problem? And how will they feel once it's been resolved?

These answers will help you get to the heart of what *really* motivates your prospects and customers.

But we're still only guessing.

That's why step three in this exercise is to actually schedule short conversations with as many of your top customers as possible and ask them these questions. Take careful notes of each conversation.

Put in the time to complete this exercise. It's one of the most valuable investments into the future of your business that you could ever make. It will result in better messaging, better marketing, and ultimately more and better customers for your business.

So as you begin to reinvent your messaging, remember that you should *not* focus on yourself, your years of experience, the awards you've won, or even how great your products and services are.

Instead, your messaging should focus on how much better your customers' lives are going to be once they do business with you!

HOW TO IDENTIFY THE RIGHT MEDIA CHANNELS TO DELIVER YOUR MESSAGE

Based on your work so far in this chapter, you've got two very valuable pieces of information:

- a crystal-clear definition of who your ideal prospects are; and
- a messaging framework that speaks to the driving factors that *really* motivate your best prospects to take action and engage your services.

Armed with this information, we can now begin considering the various media channels that are available to you in order to deliver your message to your target audience.

But first, let's take this opportunity to consider your current and past marketing campaigns. Did your marketing vendors take the time to identify your target market and think through messaging before selling you on a media campaign?

Most marketing vendors never put in this work.

Which is shocking and unfortunate—really, we consider it extreme negligence—because it means that the campaigns you spend thousands of dollars each month to run don't work nearly as well as they could work, if they even work at all.

You *have* to put in the strategic work first.

You *have* to have a clear understanding of *who* your target prospects are, and you need a carefully crafted message in order to drive them to action.

Otherwise you don't know how to calibrate your machine, and you're going to make costly mistakes.

So why don't most marketing vendors do this strategic work? A few different reasons:

They typically don't get paid for strategic work; they get paid for their service deliverables.

Most marketing vendors are trained to sell specific tools—like Google Ads or SEO—rather than building a custom strategy for their clients. You've probably heard the saying "*If all you've got is a hammer, every problem looks like a nail.*" That's how most marketing vendors operate. They've got a hammer, and they're going to try to convince you that your problem is a nail ... whether it is or it isn't.

That's why it's *your* job—with our help—to create the strategic blueprint for your Automatic Marketing Machine before engaging marketing vendors to build the machine.

And then when it's time to add a marketing vendor to your team, we recommend that you begin by reviewing our list of vetted, certified vendors, which you can access at www.AutomaticMarketing Machine.com/vendors. Or simply scan the QR code below:

So, let's talk about choosing the right media channels. Again, it's pretty simple:

Do your target prospects spend time on Facebook? Great! Try a Facebook Ads campaign.

Do your target prospects read the local newspaper? Great! Try running an ad campaign in the newspaper.

Do your target prospects listen to certain podcasts or subscribe to certain industry publications or attend specific events? Great! Try advertising there!

Pretty often, digital advertising will be the backbone of your marketing machine. That's because today's technology has made it easy and affordable to reach a very highly targeted audience.

Ads on platforms such as Facebook, LinkedIn, and even YouTube can be very effective for business owners in almost any industry. And we'll talk plenty about how to use these platforms in the coming chapters.

But don't disregard old-school marketing—like radio, print advertising, and direct mail. Many entrepreneurs all across the country are experiencing success running these types of ad campaigns even as most marketers shift their attention to digital ads.

In the next couple of chapters, we will talk about *how* to use your media channels. But before we close this chapter, we're going to share a list of some of the most popular media channels that are working for many small businesses today, along with some context for each.

This is *not* intended to be an exhaustive list; rather, this is a list intended to familiarize you with some of the most common options that you're likely to encounter in today's market.

Facebook Ads. Facebook is the largest and most dominant social media network in the United States as of this writing. Its advertising platform is very powerful. Facebook Ads allow you to target an extremely specific audience—filtering by details like zip code, family status, household income, language, hobbies, interests, and more. In addition to targeting by demographics and psychographics, Facebook also gives you the ability to import your own list of customers and prospective customers and market to them as well.

YouTube Ads. YouTube is the second most popular search engine in the United States. Millions of Americans regularly search for answers on YouTube—from DIY home improvement projects to car repairs to business advice. This makes YouTube an excellent advertising platform for many small businesses—especially because well-crafted video content is an effective channel to connect with prospects and begin developing the trust and rapport necessary to close the deal.

Google Ads. Google—and other search engines like Bing and Yahoo!—allow you to reach prospects as they are actively looking for help. For example, an accountant could program their ads to show up when somebody within their zip code searches *accounting help* or *tax strategy* or whatever other phrases make sense. This is powerful—it allows you to reach prospects at the moment when they are searching for help.

LinkedIn Ads. Similar to Facebook Ads, LinkedIn allows businesses to reach a highly targeted audience with their advertising. LinkedIn can work very well for business-to-business companies, in particular, since LinkedIn allows for very specific targeting based on business industry, size, revenue, and more.

Google Local Services Ads. Local Services Ads, or LSAs, are a new concept that Google has rolled out to certain industries in 2021. Unlike traditional search engine advertising, your business pays Google only when a lead is actually generated.

Search engine optimization. Search engine optimization, also known as SEO, is a different form of search engine advertising. Rather than directly paying Google or Bing to place ads on their search engine, SEO is focused on manipulating the organic search results so that your company website appears at the top of the rankings when somebody searches for your services.

But a word of caution about SEO. Approach with extreme caution.

There are quality SEO vendors, and there are some success stories, but most of the time SEO is *not* the first place that a small business should invest. We've both heard literally hundreds of stories about small businesses that invest hundreds and hundreds of dollars every month and never get any type of trackable return on their investment. Marketing agencies *love* to sell SEO services because it's very hard to hold them accountable. So … proceed with caution.

Remember, the list above is not intended to be exhaustive. It's an overview designed to get your brain working on this puzzle.

As always, when thinking about any marketing campaign, remember rule #10: results matter!

Facebook Ads may work for lots of businesses, but if they're not working for *your* business, don't keep shoveling good money after bad. That's why it's so important, like we've said in the previous chapters, that you're *tracking* the results of every single advertising campaign so that you know what's working and what's not.

Market. Message. Media.

Don't move past this chapter until you've got a clear picture of your target market. Don't move past this chapter until you've created a framework for compelling, customer-centric messaging. And don't move past this chapter until you've at least begun to think about a list of media channels that you can use to deliver your message to your target market.

These are the three variables that determine the success or failure of every single marketing campaign—and you have to get them right if you're serious about building an Automatic Marketing Machine that really works for your small business.

CHAPTER NINE

BUILDING YOUR LEAD GENERATION SYSTEM, PART ONE

T he first job of your Automatic Marketing Machine is to persuade your target prospects to raise their hands and identify themselves as *interested* in your products or your services. This is what we're talking about when we say "lead generation."

So what's a *lead*?

A lead is somebody that has identified themselves as interested in your products, your services, your solutions.

There are a lot of different ways somebody could become a lead for your business!

They could ...

- fill out a contact form on your website

- walk into your store or restaurant

- call your office and request a free consultation

- download a resource from your website

- sign up for your newsletter

- give you their business card and ask for more information

- attend one of your webinars

- find your booth at a trade show and sign up for a demo or a consultation

Obviously this isn't an exhaustive list. But you get the point, right? There are dozens and dozens of ways that somebody could become a lead for your business.

Let's talk about why lead generation is such a big deal.

It's a big deal because once somebody becomes a lead, you can launch your follow-up campaigns with confidence because you're not wasting your advertising dollars on prospects that aren't interested.

> **Once somebody becomes a lead, you can launch your follow-up campaigns with confidence.**

You've gotten them to raise their hands and step forward and identify themselves as interested prospects.

Basically, they're saying, "Market to me!" … and from years and years of experience, we can tell you it's a lot more profitable to market to people who have already told you that they're very interested in your products and services.

This chapter (and the next one!) is all about building your lead generation system—a series of wells, tanks, pumps, and pipes to generate leads for your business. Once you've generated the lead, of course, you'll need to have machinery in place that will allow you to *convert* the lead into a paying customer, client, diner, member, passenger, or whatever—and we'll cover that too. But let's start at the beginning, with lead generation.

There are basically two types of lead generation campaigns. Think of them as two different types of pipelines designed to bring a steady flow of leads into your business.

Pipeline number one is known as a call-me-now campaign. These are campaigns that are intended to *immediately* generate a new customer for your business. These types of campaigns are typically deployed when your business is marketing urgent or at least time-sensitive products or services.

If someone just had their car break down, for example, they don't have time to mess around. They're looking for an auto mechanic *immediately*, and a call-me-now campaign is intended to make sure they call *you* instead of the competition.

If someone has just been arrested … they need a criminal defense lawyer, and they need them right away.

Or if you're selling something to your customers that's not necessarily urgent, but your customers are still often buying on the spur of the moment—maybe you own a restaurant or a shoe store or a sporting goods store—this type of campaign is designed to reach them in their moment of decision and get them into your store quickly.

Pipeline number two is known as a funnel or a lead-nurture campaign. While a call-me-now campaign is intended to attract customers who need your products and services *now*, a funnel campaign is meant to attract prospects who aren't facing urgent pressure to make a decision.

These prospects are typically *starting to think* about hiring an accountant or a lawyer or a psychiatrist or a chiropractor.

They're perhaps conducting some research, doing their due diligence, but not quite ready to pick up the phone and schedule an appointment.

A business owner who's growing quickly and is ready to hire an accountant to help with taxes. An unhappy spouse starting to think about divorce. Parents who have a child starting to show signs of possible depression. A middle-aged man who is starting to experience back pain. Basically, situations where the prospect is going to take some time and do some research before choosing a service provider rather than picking up the phone and making an appointment right away.

These are the type of situations where a lead-nurture campaign can be very valuable.

Neither of these campaigns is wrong or right—neither is inherently better than the other. Rather, these are two distinct tools with very different use cases. If you try to use a lead-nurture campaign with a prospect who needs help immediately, you're going to lose them because they need fast action and they don't have time to mess around.

On the other hand, if you try to use a call-me-now campaign with a prospect who is not in a rush and who is not ready to make a buying decision, you're going to lose them because they're not ready to commit.

These are two different tools in your tool kit. In this chapter, we're going to take a deep dive into call-me-now campaigns, and next chapter we'll do the same with lead-nurture campaigns.

HOW TO DEVELOP A WINNING CALL-ME-NOW CAMPAIGN

By the end of this chapter, you should be able to write and deploy a simple call-me-now campaign across at least three different media channels.

The formula for a profitable call-me-now campaign is very straightforward. It's essentially a four-part formula. Later, after you get your four-part formula working, you can experiment with more complex formulas, but for now let's keep it simple so you can get some quick wins.

Here's the formula:

1. Identify the person—or more specifically, help your prospect identify themselves.

2. Identify the problem.

3. Present the solution.

4. Give them a call to action so they don't have to wonder how to solve their problem.

For example,

1. Are you an entrepreneur, or do you own a small business?

2. Are you sick and tired of wondering where your next prospective new customers are going to come from, when they're going to come, and even if they're going to come?

3. Building an Automatic Marketing Machine could be just the solution for you because it helps entrepreneurs and small business owners produce a steady, predictable stream of highly qualified prospects, day in and day out, so that you don't have to worry anymore about where your next customer is going to come from.

(Now just imagine how you would feel if we didn't give you a call to action at this point. You'd probably be pretty frustrated! That's why we always insist that every advertisement we ask our clients to invest their money on includes a trackable and measurable call to action.)

4. So if you are an entrepreneur or you own a small business, you are sick and tired of wondering where and when your next prospect is going to show up, and you would like to build a simple call-me-now campaign so that you can generate prospects consistently, keep reading or listening because that's what we're about to show you how to do before this chapter is over.

Simple and straightforward.

Do you identify with this description?

Do you have this kind of problem or opportunity?

Does this kind of solution appeal to you?

Here's something you can do about it!

None of this is rocket science! But most marketing vendors screw it up because they don't do the strategic work that we covered last chapter—mapping out the market, message, media fit.

So you're going to develop your four-part message, which speaks to your ideal market and gives them clear instructions about what you want them to do next.

Now let's talk about the media.

To keep things simple, we're going to walk you through how to create a very basic three-channel call-me-now media campaign. As you're about to see, it's called a three-channel media campaign because we're going to deploy it across three different media channels.

But just because it's simple, don't for one second think it can't start generating business for you right away. So for purposes of this exercise, we're going to focus on Facebook, LinkedIn, and YouTube.

We're going to assume that you already have a Facebook account, a LinkedIn account, and a YouTube channel. And we are going to assume that you know how to make posts on your Facebook and

LinkedIn accounts and that you know how to shoot a short video on your phone and then upload it to your YouTube channel.

If you need help with any of this, please scan the QR code or visit www.AutomaticMarketingMachine.com/tutorials for guided step-by-step instructions.

So here we go:

Step one: Describe one of your ideal target prospects. Don't try to describe everyone—let's just focus on one particular type of prospect.

Here are a few examples of how to do this:

- Do you own a law firm grossing less than one million dollars?

- Are you a restaurateur looking to double the revenues of your restaurant in the next twelve months?

- Do you own the best shoe store in town, but you're frustrated that it's also the best-kept secret in town?

Work the first part of your formula out for yourself. (If you'd like a worksheet to guide you through this process, just visit www.AutomaticMarketingMachine.com/4PartFormula and download it. Or scan the QR code below.)

In **step two** we are going to say something that causes your ideal prospect to self-identify and say to themselves, *"It sounds like they might be describing me; I should probably pay attention."*

So let's describe a very specific problem that your ideal prospect is currently looking for a solution to.

Sticking with our examples of the law firm owner, the restaurateur, and the owner of the best shoe store in town, let's now describe a very specific problem each of them might be losing sleep over at this very moment. Remember, this is a call-me-now campaign. We'll talk about what you're going to want to do differently in a nurture campaign, and why, in the next chapter.

- Are you the owner of a law firm grossing less than one million dollars? Do you sometimes find yourself regretting that you accepted an engagement from a crazy client, but the only reason you did so is because you didn't have enough confidence in your firm's marketing to turn down the work?

- Are you a restaurateur looking to double the revenues of your restaurant in the next twelve months? Are you sick and tired of buying customers one at a time with expensive advertising that eats up all your profits?

- Do you own the best shoe store in town, but you're frustrated that it's also the best-kept secret? Are you losing sleep over the prospect of having to close your doors forever if you can't bring in a steady stream of customers—and soon?

Step three: Present the solution.

- Are you the owner of a law firm grossing less than one million dollars? Do you sometimes find yourself regretting that you accepted an engagement from a crazy client, but the only reason you did so is because you didn't have enough confidence in your law firm's marketing to turn down the work? **An Automatic Marketing Machine is simple to build, profitable to run, and can give you the confidence you need to decline work from the next crazy client who contacts your firm.**

- Are you a restaurateur looking to double the revenues of your restaurant in the next twelve months? Are you sick and tired of buying customers one at a time with expensive advertising that eats up all your profits? **An Automatic Marketing Machine is simple to build, profitable to run, and brings your best customers back again and again.**

- Do you own the best shoe store in town, but you're frustrated that it's also the best-kept secret? Are you losing sleep over the prospect of having to close your doors forever if you can't bring in a steady stream of customers—and soon? **An Automatic Marketing Machine is simple to build and profitable to run, and if you'll let it work for you, you might be surprised just how quickly it can start bringing in a steady stream of new customers.**

Step four: Now that we've got their attention and raised their hopes, we need to add a call to action. Let's not leave them to their own devices to figure out what to do next.

- Are you the owner of a law firm grossing less than one million dollars? Do you sometimes find yourself regretting that you accepted an engagement from a crazy client, but the only reason you did so is because you didn't have enough confidence in your law firm's marketing to turn down the work? An Automatic Marketing Machine is simple to build, profitable to run, and can give you the confidence you need to decline work from the next crazy client who contacts your firm. **Visit www.AutomaticMarketingMachine.com/lawyers to buy your copy of** *The Automatic Marketing Machine for Lawyers.*

- Are you a restaurateur looking to double the revenues of your restaurant in the next twelve months? Are you sick and tired of buying customers one at a time with expensive advertising that eats up all your profits? An Automatic Marketing Machine is simple to build, profitable to run, and brings your best customers back again and again. **Please visit www. AutomaticMarketingMachine.com/restaurants to place your order for** *The Automatic Marketing Machine for Restaurants.*

- Do you own the best shoe store in town, but you're frustrated that it's also the best-kept secret? Are you losing sleep over the prospect of having to close your doors forever if you can't bring in a steady stream of customers—and soon? An Automatic Marketing Machine is simple to build and profitable to run, and if you'll let it work for you, you might be surprised just how quickly it can start bringing in a steady stream of new customers. **Scan this QR code to request your copy of** *The Automatic Marketing Machine for Retailers.*

Congratulations, you've just written your first call-me-now ad!

Log on to your Facebook account, and post it!

Log on to your LinkedIn account, and post it!

Pull out your phone, and record a short video using your ad as the script. Then, log on to your YouTube account and upload it!

Once you've got your ads posted, tag us (The Automatic Marketing Machine) so everyone who follows us will find your ad.

That's called boosting your ad for free without giving money to a marketing vendor. And then after you're done boosting your ad by tagging us—you're welcome very much!—find other places where your prospects hang out, like Facebook and LinkedIn groups, and share your posts there too!

Congratulations, you've just launched your first call-me-now campaign ... don't be surprised if it starts getting you some business!

In the next chapter, we'll talk through the second lead generation pipeline that you can use to generate qualified leads for your business.

CHAPTER TEN

BUILDING YOUR LEAD GENERATION SYSTEM, PART TWO

n the previous chapter, we introduced the concept of lead generation, and we talked about two very different types of lead generation pipelines that you can use to pump a steady flow of prospects into your business.

A call-me-now campaign—which is meant to quickly generate leads for your business.

And a lead-nurture campaign, which generates, nurtures, and delivers leads for your business over a longer period of time.

If you followed our instructions in the last chapter … you've already launched a simple call-me-now campaign.

Now you might be wondering, Why would I want anything other than a call-me-now campaign?

Isn't business now better than business later?

Well, yes, duh! And there are a lot of businesses that benefit from effective call-me-now campaigns!

But there are other types of businesses where call-me-now campaigns actually create more problems than they solve. Problems like …

- too many unqualified prospects

- prospects that don't show up for their appointments

- prospects that are price shopping and only looking for the cheapest possible solution

- prospects that are assholes to you and your staff

- prospects that waste your time but don't end up buying anything

If these are the issues you're running into, then a lead-nurture campaign is probably the solution you need.

A lead-nurture campaign means that instead of asking your audience to immediately call you and schedule a consultation, you provide them with some sort of **free tool or resource** that will be helpful as they consider their next steps, and then you nurture them along their journey.

This resource, which is often called a lead magnet, could be a free e-book, a checklist, a webinar, a video lesson, or just about anything else that has value to your prospects.

You offer this resource for free to your prospects—but you ask for their contact information in exchange. Once you've got this information, you can automatically trigger a follow-up campaign, which we'll discuss in depth in the next chapter.

For example, if you're a family law firm specializing in divorce, you could create a lead magnet addressing topics like …

- how to tell your spouse you want a divorce

- how to get divorced without harming your kids in the process

- how to plan your finances during and after divorce

- how to tell your family that you're getting divorced

And so on. You could deliver this content in written form as a free guide, special report, white paper, or e-book, or in a similar format. Or you could deliver it in video format or even using a webinar.

The key, in order to make a campaign like this successful, is that you create a resource that is legitimately valuable to your prospects—that speaks to a real concern or pain point that they're experiencing.

Even though you're offering it for free, your prospects aren't going to give you their contact information unless you can convince them that your lead magnet is legitimately valuable to them.

Here are some pointers for creating an effective lead magnet and making it work:

Create a resource that solves a real, specific problem for your prospects. This is why the exercise of interviewing your best customers, which we went through two chapters ago, is so valuable. You don't have to guess at the problems and the pain points they're experiencing—you know. Get as specific as you can!

Speak to their real motivations. Remember, your prospects don't wake up in the morning excited to go spend money on your products and services. They do business with you because they have a problem or opportunity in their life and they need your help to deal with it. So don't talk about how great your products and services are. Instead speak to their emotions, their pain points, their stress. Speak to their hopes, plans, and aspirations.

Don't overwhelm with too much information. Lots of business owners go overboard in a well-intentioned effort to provide value to prospects. But remember, your prospects are human beings living in the twenty-first century—which means they're busy, distracted, and probably overwhelmed just trying to make it through the day. They just don't have the ability or desire to understand the details of your products and services. So don't overwhelm them. Offer them a resource that solves a clear, specific problem with a limited scope. Don't tell them how the sausage is made ... just give it to them!

Create a landing page that persuasively sells the benefits of your lead magnet. Even though you're giving it away for free, you have to make a compelling case as to why your prospects should give you their contact information. Help them understand how this resource is going to solve at least one pressing problem and make their life better as a result.

Remember, your lead magnet can take many different forms. For example, your lead magnet could be a:

- free resource

- e-book

- guide

- checklist

- video lesson

- webinar

- live event

- workbook

And so on. Experiment with different formats, and see what performs best. You're going to have to test multiple lead magnets, and you're going to want to test them on multiple media channels.

Remember, building your Automatic Marketing Machine is an incremental process—it's not going to happen overnight. It's going to require testing and tinkering. Embrace it!

> If you want detailed, step-by-step instructions and work-sheets that guide you through the process of building a lead-nurture campaign, we've got that for you! Just visit www.AutomaticMarketingMachine.com/LeadNurture to download the materials. Or scan the QR code here:

Right about now, you might be wondering … "What am I supposed to do with my prospects who download my lead magnet?"

That's where the real magic happens in a lead-nurture campaign. And that, dear readers, is what the next chapter is all about!

CHAPTER ELEVEN

BUILDING YOUR LEAD CONVERSION SYSTEM

"Not following up with your prospects is the same as filling up your bathtub without first putting the stopper in the drain."
—MICHELLE MOORE

B y now you understand the importance of building an Automatic Marketing Machine.

You understand why it's so important that you stop hauling leaky buckets back and forth from the river all day.

You're starting to see why it's such a game changer when you have an Automatic Marketing Machine working for you, delivering a steady and predictable stream of qualified prospects for your business.

You understand—or you can imagine—how much better life is going to become once you have the confidence to decline working with prospects that aren't a good fit, because you have a marketing machine that you're confident in.

You've learned why market, message, media fit is so important, and you've gone through exercises not only to help you get clear on *who* your ideal prospects are but also on the messaging you'll use to attract them.

You've learned why lead generation is the essential first step in your marketing machine.

And you understand the difference between a call-me-now campaign, which is designed to quickly generate leads at a high volume, and a lead-nurture campaign, which is designed to weed out the prospects that aren't a good fit and deliver the prospects who *are* a good fit for your business.

Up until now, we've been focused on getting the prospect to raise their hand and identify themselves as a lead who's worth investing your valuable time, energy, and money to convert into an actual paying customer.

Think of it this way: the water starts in the river, then it gets sucked up into the pipeline, then it has to get accelerated and transported to the village until it finally comes out of the faucet, when it can be put to productive use.

The point of all this is to get the water out of the faucet and put it to productive use.

If it leaks out of the pipeline before it gets to the village, if the faucet never gets turned on, or if it comes out of the faucet and just goes down the drain, then it has failed.

Remember the only question that really matters … *Does it work?*

In other words, sticking with our analogy, was the water useful for bathing, or cooking, or drinking, or for irrigating crops?

If all we did was construct a pipeline to extract water from a river and pump it through pipes and valves through the jungle to come out of the faucet on the other end, but it doesn't get put to productive use, well, that's a fascinating engineering feat, but it's not what we're here to do.

We're here to create a steady stream of prospects so that you can grow your business.

And that's why in this chapter, we're going to focus on building your lead conversion system—that is, developing a follow-up system to take a lead (someone who has raised their hand) and deliver them to your sales team for a consultation or a strategy session or an assessment or whatever the next step looks like in your new-customer onboarding process.

This is where your lead conversion system—one of the most important parts of your Automatic Marketing Machine—comes into play.

The purpose of your lead conversion system is to ensure that as many of your qualified leads as possible **take the next step** toward doing business with you ... again, that could be scheduling a consultation, appointment, or strategy session ... or it might just mean showing up in your storefront! And don't forget, your lead conversion system is also meant to serve as a filter—you don't want muddy water coming out of the faucet!

Goals of your lead conversion system include

- ensuring that qualified prospects actually *show up* for their appointment or their visit,

- ensuring that *unqualified* prospects are weeded out prior to their appointment or visit so that they don't show up and waste everyone's time,

- ensuring that prospects arrive in the right *frame of mind* for their meeting or visit, and

- preconditioning your prospects to work with *your team*—not just you. Otherwise you've simply created a job for yourself.

This requires a step-by-step follow-up system, which is to be triggered immediately after the prospect becomes a lead.

And the system will look different if the lead was generated through a call-me-now campaign as opposed to a lead-nurture campaign.

To go back to our pipeline analogy, you don't need to engineer as much screening and filtration and purification if you're just using the water to irrigate crops as you do if you're using the water to cook and drink.

How to Follow Up on a Call-Me-Now Campaign

If the lead was generated through a call-me-now campaign, the conversion process is pretty quick and simple because the prospect will have already scheduled a consultation or visited your location, usually within a day or two of the first contact.

However, you should still deliver at least one communication to these leads *after* they've scheduled their appointment but *before* they actually show up.

Because of the compressed timeframe, this will probably be an automated email and/or text message.

This communication should include the following ingredients:

- a reminder that you understand their true motivations in seeking your help—the fear, the stress, the excitement, the emotions that drove your prospect to reach out to you

- encouragement and optimism to help them see the light at the end of the tunnel even if their current circumstances are difficult

- social proof to instill confidence that your business has helped many other people just like them

- an idea of what to expect during their appointment or their visit so that fear of the unknown doesn't hold them back

- all the logistic details they'll need: how to find your location (or your Zoom link if the consultation will take place virtually), where to park, who to call if they get lost or have trouble connecting to Zoom, etc.

(By the way, we've built a template for this preconsultation email which you can download and customize for your business. Scan the QR code or visit www.AutomaticMarketingMachine.com/Conversion *to get your template!)*

Once you've created the messaging for this communication, it's very important that you *automate* it so that it happens, consistently, without you having to lift a finger.

There's a reason we're building an *Automatic* Marketing Machine—because we don't want you to get stuck manually turning a crank all day, every day.

Most of the customer relationship management software programs you'll find in today's market offer this functionality, and in addition there are many simple and affordable email marketing programs that offer this functionality as well. Two of our favorite email automation systems are Mailchimp and ActiveCampaign.

How to Develop Killer Follow-Up for Your Lead-Nurture Campaigns

Following up on your lead-nurture campaigns is a little bit more complicated—because your prospects haven't yet scheduled an appointment, and some of them are weeks or even months away from being ready to do so.

But building a robust follow-up system is also one of the biggest opportunities for your business simply because the vast majority of your competitors out there simply are not doing it. And the ones that are doing it … are generally doing it poorly.

All of which means that your lead conversion system will become a huge competitive advantage for your business. Or to be even more direct, it will make you a whole lot of money if you do this right!

So let's map it out.

The conversion system kicks off as soon as someone raises their hand and identifies themselves as a lead for your business.

Let's carry on our example from the last chapter and assume that you own a family law firm and your prospects have downloaded a lead magnet entitled "How to Get Divorced without Screwing Up Your Kids."

The very first step is to deliver the PDF that the prospect requested. This requires a very simple automation that can be easily created within your customer relationship management system or just about any email marketing program.

Create a short, simple message that looks something like this:

Hi [first name]!

Here's the resource you requested—"How to Get Divorced without Screwing Up Your Kids." Just click here for your instant download.

If you have any problems accessing this resource, please reply to this email and let me know.

I know how overwhelming it can feel to think about getting divorced. Nobody gets married expecting it to end this way, and it's even more complicated when you have children involved.

Here's the good news: my team and I have worked with hundreds of families just like yours over the last ten years, and I can assure you that there is a light at the end of the tunnel. It really does get easier. It might feel like life is ending right now—but there is an exciting new beginning for you and your family right around the corner.

Please reach out if you have any questions. And if you'd like to talk to our family law team about your plans and your concerns, simply click here to request a consultation.

—[Your signature]

Again, this should all be automated so that it's delivered immediately without requiring manual labor. This is especially important with a campaign like this because often a prospect is doing their research on the internet outside of normal working hours. If they have to wait until Monday morning to get the resource they've requested, it'll be too late.

Notice the balance we struck with this messaging. You don't want to be pushy or aggressive with this type of follow-up. Your prospect has requested information, and the purpose of this follow-up email is to provide them with the information they requested.

But you would be doing yourself and your prospect a disservice if you did not begin to tell them about the solution you've built that will solve the problem that they are facing.

So *every single communication* in your follow-up sequence needs to include a call to action for them to take the next step—whether that's scheduling a meeting, requesting a strategy session, or visiting your store … whatever the case may be.

> **Every single communication in your follow-up sequence needs to include a call to action.**

Now let's talk about the rest of your follow-up sequence. The basic premise is simple: assume that your leads, like most people, are busy, distracted, and stressed out.

There's never enough time in the day for them to accomplish everything on their to-do lists.

Further, assume that your leads, like most people, shy away from making major decisions and major changes in their lives because they're naturally fearful of the unknown.

All of this means that you have a *lot of work to do* if you're going to break through and drive them to take action. Which means that one follow-up message is *not* enough.

At minimum, you should have a five-step follow-up sequence for your leads. We know … five seems like overkill! We used to think so too. But thanks to decades of testing, we can tell you that a five-step follow-up sequence works exponentially better than a one-, two-, or even three-step follow-up sequence.

The math typically works out something like this: let's say you invest $10 per lead to get 100 leads. You have invested $1,000. You'll probably get around a 2 to 3 percent response rate to your first follow-up. Assuming your sales process works really well, that's going to get you two to three new customers. For purposes of this example, let's just say your average customer is worth $1,000. If you're selling professional services, that number is probably much higher; if you are selling donuts and you have a solid earn-back campaign, which we'll talk about in chapter 12 of this book, that number is probably much higher for you, too, because once someone buys one donut from your shop, you'll learn how to get them to come back again and again, make referrals, and bring their friends.

So you've invested $1,000, you've done a one-step follow-up campaign, and it's brought you between $2,000 and $3,000 of business. Not bad. In fact this is what most business owners would consider to be a home run. But if you were like most business owners, you wouldn't be reading this book. So let's say you turn up the dial way past where most other business owners stop, and you build a three-step follow-up campaign that boosts your response rate to around 4 to 5 percent. That's 4 to 5 percent total. You got 2 to 3 percent on the first touch and 1 to 2 percent more on the second and third follow-ups.

This boosts your sales to around $4,000 on that same $1,000 lead-gen spend, which, if you do the math, is actually 100 percent more ROI than if you settle for a one-step follow-up. Now, there will tend to be some diminishing returns between follow-ups four and five, but it is not at all unusual to see a pickup of 1 more percent, which, using the math from our example, is another $1,000, for a grand total of around $5,000 on a $1,000 ad spend.

Either way, you're spending the same $1,000 to get the same 100 leads. The business with one follow-up will get a 200 to 300 percent ROI, and the business that follows up five times will get a 500 percent

ROI. That's $2,000 of additional sales on each $1,000 spent on the same advertisement.

But there's more!

Let's suppose the business in question has a 50 percent gross profit margin. That's $1,000 of additional gross profit on that same $1,000 ad spend. Which means those four extra follow-up steps effectively drop your cost of acquisition to zero when compared to the same business settling for just one follow-up.

Some people reading this book have a really good handle on the finances and the bookkeeping of their business, and you're probably getting really excited about this revelation.

(If you aren't grinning ear to ear at this point, please scan the QR code below or visit www.bookkeepingthatdoesntsuck.com/AMM for a free report to help you find more profits in your business.)

So yes, you need to follow up at least five times on your leads. And here are three more important tips as you begin to build out your lead-nurture pipeline:

- Don't limit yourself only to email. Consider other forms of follow-up as well, such as physical mail, text messaging, social media, or even a phone call.

- Deliver *value* in every follow-up—give them a reason to stay engaged so they don't tune you out.

- Include a strong call to action every single time. Position your products or services as the solution to the problem or opportunity that they're facing, and make it clear and simple for them to take the next step.

Now, let's map out the rest of the follow-up sequence for our family law firm. You can modify this and use it for your own business, no matter what industry you're in.

- **Email one**: Instant response, delivering the resource that the prospect requested. (This is the email we've already reviewed earlier in this chapter.)

- **Email two**: Send two days after the first email, following up to ensure the prospect got the resource, asking if they have any questions, and providing a link to schedule their appointment or visit your store.

- **Email three**: Send three days later, offering another piece of helpful content—such as a blog entry or a video. Also include a link to schedule their visit to your location.

- **Email four**: Send three days later, sharing testimonials and success stories designed to help the prospect begin to create a vision for how much better life could look once they purchase your products or services. Include a link to schedule their visit.

- **Email five**: Send three days later, sharing a blog, infographic, article, or video that will be helpful to the prospect. And include a link to schedule their visit.

- After email five, add the prospect to your main mailing list so that they continue to receive your newsletters and other communications.

You're probably wondering, Why did we choose the magic number of five follow-up emails? And how did we determine the timing between each email?

There's nothing magic about the number five. It's a good place to start—much better than the average business, which doesn't follow up at all or follows up just once.

But there's no reason you can't build a longer follow-up sequence when you're ready to do so.

The delay between each follow-up is something that you need to experiment with as well. Start with your best guess and adjust accordingly based on actual performance.

Remember that you can scan the QR code or visit www.Automatic MarketingMachine.com/KPIs to download a simple KPI tracker that will help you make sense of all this!

At this point you might be thinking … this all sounds great, but I have no idea how to write follow-up messages that will actually get my prospects to take action.

Good news: it's *much* more simple than you probably realize.

Why Writing Copy to Sell When Following Up Is Actually Very Simple

Here's how to write copy that sells like a rock star, and it's really, really simple.

Are you ready?

Charles Dickens has already written the best book on selling like a rock star that's ever been written. You've already read it. Studied it.

Written essays about it. Maybe even performed in it for the school play. You've all seen the movies and the adaptations of the movies and the derivations of the movies.

The book: *A Christmas Carol.*

Now, when most people write sales copy, they write copy that sounds like the Ghost of Christmas Past—telling their clients and customers all the things they've already messed up.

That never works.

Instead, you want to write copy and sell like the Ghost of Christmas Future—helping your prospects see what's coming if they *do* versus what's coming if they *don't* change their ways.

That's it.

You can sell millions of dollars of services, products, experiences, anything if you just sell like the Ghost of Christmas Future—by having the courage to care enough about your prospects to help them see what's coming if they do versus if they don't change their trajectory.

But that's not the way most business owners would prefer to do it. The way most business owners would prefer to do it is to cite all kinds of technical details and talk about why their products and services are so much better than the competition.

But that's not where the prospect finds the urgency to make the decisions they need to make in order to do something about their future. And unless you can invent a time machine, bring them back to the past to fix the mistake they've already made, and undo it, there ain't nothing you can do to change that, and rubbing their nose in it isn't going to make them want to do business with you.

Instead, write your copy to help them make sense of their situation and understand what's likely to happen if they go down the left fork in the road versus the right versus just standing there at the point of decision forever while the rest of the world leaves them behind.

Essentially, tell them, "This is what's probably going on in your life right now if you have this kind of problem. This is what's probably going to happen. These are your options. These are the likely consequences," and help them make a decision about which course of action is going to be more impactful for them. That's what selling in person and selling in print is all about.

It really is this simple.

A Secret Weapon to Make All Your Follow-Up More Effective

What if there was a secret weapon guaranteed to make all your follow-up marketing work better and therefore guaranteed to provide more prospects, more customers, and more revenue for your business?

Well, there is: **video**.

Video is statistically the most effective communication medium available today—and it's not even close. Video creates a human connection with your prospects in a way that nothing else can replicate.

And so incorporating video into your advertising campaigns and *especially* into your lead conversion system will make them perform even better.

Remember, one of the biggest obstacles to overcome when driving your prospects to take the next step toward doing business with you … is the fear of the unknown that they're facing.

Video is a great tool to develop rapport with your prospects and help them feel comfortable with the situation that they're going to walk in to.

Your lead conversion system is absolutely essential to the success of your Automatic Marketing Machine.

Without an effective follow-up system, you're leaving money on the table. If you look closely enough, a strong lead conversion system is at the heart of virtually every successful marketing campaign in any industry you can imagine!

It's not sexy, it's not exciting—but it works.

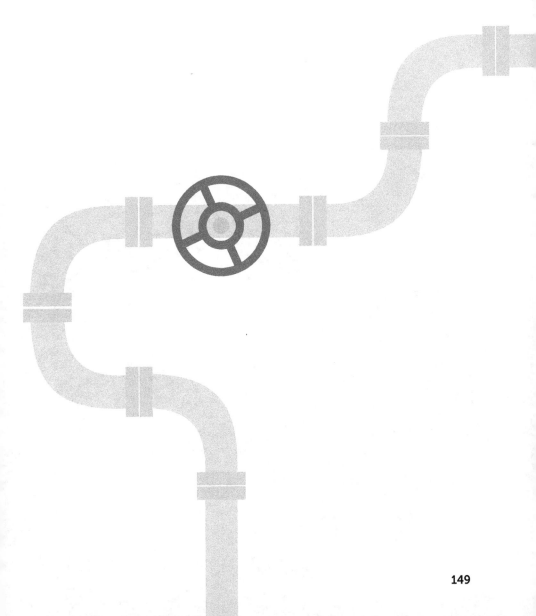

CHAPTER TWELVE

MAXIMIZING CUSTOMER LIFETIME VALUE

This is the part of the puzzle that hardly anyone else is doing. But you can! And hopefully, you will. Because this is the part that can quickly and easily give you a *huge* unfair competitive advantage. In this chapter we're going to help you understand how to maximize the lifetime value of each new customer who engages your business, turning one engagement into a series of engagements and one customer into two, thus increasing the value of every new customer exponentially!

Which of course means you can give yourself an enormous competitive marketing advantage. Just imagine what it means for your marketing budget when each new customer is worth four times more to your business than any other. And best of all, this is the easiest system to implement in your business.

One of the most important keys to maximizing the lifetime value of a customer of your business is to think in terms of lifetime value, not transactional value, unlike most entrepreneurs. Most business owners are out there trying to get a customer so they can squeeze work out of the customer. The Automatic Marketing Machine turns that on its head and has us looking for any opportunity to do something of value for a person—even if it's for free—in order to *earn the right* to call that person a customer.

Imagine you own a widget factory. It could be a professional services firm, a retail store, a restaurant, a manufacturing operation … it could be anything. Imagine that you and all your so-called competitors sell a more or less comparable product, with the same cost of goods sold, for about the same price.

And you all have the same basic challenge: your prospects don't know how much better their life will be with your product or service, and so they delay, they procrastinate, they look for cheaper and inferior options, not even realizing that they are inferior. They're basically out there struggling with their problem or missing out on a great opportunity because they don't know what they don't know … because they've never had a taste of how much better life could be.

Now, based on the cost of goods sold, everyone in the market decides they can't afford to spend more than one dollar to acquire that same customer that everyone is competing to get.

Then, all of a sudden, someone enters the market with a plan to ensure that every new customer comes back again and again and makes referrals. And this new competitor is so confident in their Automatic Marketing Machine that they're willing to make a little bit less profit on the first sale because they know they have a system that will cause a second sale and a third sale and a fourth sale, with virtually no additional cost of acquisition.

You can probably see that this competitor has a very unfair advantage, because this competitor can amortize the cost of acquisition across two, three, four, or even five transactions.

So this competitor doesn't mind spending, or really <u>investing</u>, a bit more to acquire that revenue stream because this competitor with the Automatic Marketing Machine is thinking and calculating in terms of lifetime value, not merely transactional value.

This competitor might even be willing to lower the barrier of entry into a long-term relationship for the prospect by offering the first taste for free.

Just imagine what it could do for your business if everyone in your market was willing to spend only one dollar to make a sale, but now that you have a reliable system for turning that one sale into two and then three and turning that one customer into a referral source, now you are willing to invest two dollars to make a sale!

That's twice as much as everyone else is willing to spend. Can't you see how and why having an Automatic Marketing Machine that maximizes the lifetime value of your customers would give you such a devastatingly unfair advantage?

That's why it's so highly profitable to invest in building out a system that maintains top-of-mind awareness and keeps your business relevant in the lives of all the individuals and businesses who trusted you enough to do business with you.

Not to mention, we just think it is a matter of common decency to keep in touch with a person who has demonstrated trust in you by purchasing a product or service from your business.

So let's talk about how to make it all happen.

How to Stay Relevant with Your Past Customers and Referral Sources

Keeping your business top of mind requires your business to remain relevant. And you remain relevant by asking the right questions at the right times.

And here's the really good news … *you* are in a unique position to know what the right questions are and when to ask them. That's because if you've been in business for any substantive amount of time, you already know what's likely to happen in the lives of your customers after they do business with you!

> **You remain relevant by asking the *right questions* at the right times.**

For example:

If you sell someone a new car … you know they're going to need insurance too. And you know that statistically speaking, in about two years, they're going to start thinking about what their *next* new car is going to be.

If you help someone buy a new home … you know that right away they're probably going to be looking for a mover. And you know that within a few weeks, they're going to be looking for furniture. And you know that within a few months, they're going to be looking for a handyman to do some projects around the house.

If you help someone file their taxes … you know that in about nine months or so, they're going to start thinking about organizing their records to get ready for next year's taxes.

If you help someone get divorced … you know they're probably going to be looking for a new place to live pretty much immediately … and you know that statistically speaking, many men are going to start thinking about buying a new truck around six to nine months after the divorce is finalized, and many women are going to start thinking about cosmetic surgery around twelve to eighteen months after the divorce. No, this isn't politically correct. But it's the truth.

So here's a valuable exercise:

Think about *your* customers. Put yourself in their shoes, and think about what's likely to happen in their lives after they do business with you the first time. Write down the answers, and write down approximately when each need, problem, or opportunity is likely to arise. Hopefully this is based on your real-life observations, but if you haven't been paying attention … now you know why it's so important that you *start* paying attention to your customers' lives even after they've done business with you.

Then you need to be proactive about staying relevant and staying in touch with your customers by showing up at the right times. To your customers this is going to seem like a coincidence … and of course, without a system it will obviously become random and labor intensive—or more to the point, it will become random and inconsistent.

But this is why we are building an Automatic Marketing Machine. So that these good ideas get implemented systematically without a lot of manual labor from you. That's how we can depend on the system to work reliably, predictably, day after day, month after month, all year long.

So let's not do like most small business owners do and just sit around waiting for the phone to ring while flattering ourselves, thinking: "If any of my customers from the past need anything, including more of my products and services or even a referral, certainly they'll know to ask. Because after all, I'm so great, and I went to such-and-such school, and I have all this fancy equipment and all these years of experience and the best recipe in town for making sausages."

You already know that's not how it works in the real world!

You've already had the experience of seeing one of your former customers or clients whom you did a great job for, delivering a great product or a great service and at a great value too … you've already had the experience of seeing them doing business with someone else instead of you, and you've wondered, "How did that happen?"

You may have even allowed your ego to make up a story about how dumb, how disloyal, how unfair, how unappreciative that former customer or client is because they didn't make it their business to go out of their way to keep your contact information at the ready and the name of your business at the top of their mind.

Well, before we go casting aspersions on any of our former customers or clients, and before we go and accuse any of our competitors of not playing fair, let's be honest with ourselves. We've all been that customer. We've all been that client. We've all had a perfectly adequate experience or even a great experience with a business, but then the next time we have a need, we take the first solution offered to us.

And when is the last time anyone who ever sold you a product or provided you with any kind of service demonstrated enough care or concern for you to say:

"I have enough experience here to know that, since you're buying this product or service today, you might also need help with this other thing in the future. And because I care about my customers, I've taken it upon myself to do the research for you, and so if you ever need help with this, please let me know so I can save you a lot of time and energy and make a referral for you."

Pretty rare, right?

So at this point you have a strategic choice to make. Are you going to wait around for your customers to remember to call you, or are you going to take control of your future and build a system that keeps your business top of mind and relevant in the lives of your best customers?

Eventually, your back-end marketing system will evolve into a very sophisticated machine that will produce hundreds of thousands of dollars of repeat and referral revenue for your business every year, and if you're of a mind to do so, then millions of dollars of repeat and referral revenue to your business every quarter!

But we have to start somewhere.

And four of the quickest, easiest, and most cost-effective earn-back campaigns you can use to consistently generate repeat business and referrals include GAS calls, monthly newsletters, targeted social media campaigns, and good old-fashioned direct mail.

Let's break them down.

LIFETIME VALUE MAXIMIZING SYSTEM #1: GAS CALLS

Here's a quick strategy to massively increase your repeat and referral business—and usually generate some short-term cash flow as well.

We call this strategy *GAS calls*—GAS stands for "give a shit." As in, you're not just a number to us; we actually give a shit about you as a human being.

Yes … it's all based on the idea that your customers have lives and business interests that extend far beyond just the products and services they consume from you. So we pick up the phone, and we call our former customers with an opening that goes a little something like this:

"Hello is this [*name*]? Hi, this is [*your name*].

"It's been about a year / six months / two years / three months [*or:* It's getting toward the end of the year / It's the start of a new year], and we like to check in with our customers at around this time to go over some things that many of our customers tell us come up around this time. Do you have about twenty to thirty minutes to go over some things I'd like to check in with you about now, or can we schedule a call for another time?"

Then, when they've got time to talk, we ask them how they're doing in relation to the specific issues, concerns, or challenges we know that they're likely to be facing around this time.

And we really listen. Because we really do give a shit! Now, obviously, this is going to work a lot better if you really do give a shit about your customers—which we are going to presume you do, or you probably wouldn't have made it this far into our book, because to borrow a lesson from the last chapter, we've been filtering out the assholes since the first page of this book.

That's right: part of the reason we wrote this book is because we practice what we preach, and it serves as a wonderful lead generation magnet as well as a filtration device to accelerate the right kinds of prospects to us and protect our team from business owners who don't genuinely care about their customers and clients like we care about our clients.

So we're going to ask your customers about the specific issues, concerns, problems, or opportunities that we *know* they're likely thinking about because we've seen these issues, concerns, problems, and opportunities come up over and over again for our customers!

You should come to these calls prepared with *solutions* for the issues that you know from experience you're going to be hearing about over and over again from your customers.

(By the way, if you don't know what issues you're going to hear about from your customers, then these calls will be especially valuable for you because you're going to learn a lot and probably uncover a lot of opportunities to deliver even more services, sell more products, book more reservations, crack more backs, cut more hair, etc., etc.)

Sometimes these calls will help you uncover additional products or services you can sell to your customers.

But lots of times, the result may be a referral to another business that you trust, that you've vetted, and that you know is going to solve the problem for them.

Or you might end up offering them a free resource—like a PDF or a video lesson that walks them through the problem they're facing and helps them solve it.

Now ... when is the last time that another business owner has made a call like this to *you*?

Has it ever happened? Probably not!

At least not very often ... because most businesses don't take advantage of this simple, kind, and *profitable* strategy to show their customers that they actually give a shit about them ... even after the transaction is over.

That's good news for *you*—because when you put this practice into action as part of the Automatic Marketing Machine we're building together ... you'll stand out from the crowd like a purple unicorn, and you'll make a *lot* more money as a result.

By the way—you can visit www.AutomaticMarketingMachine.com/GAS to download sample GAS call scripts that you can modify and use for your business! Or scan the QR code below:

LIFETIME VALUE MAXIMIZING SYSTEM #2: MONTHLY NEWSLETTER

We know—this isn't sexy. But it just works.

A monthly email newsletter is very simple, low cost, and effective. It's an easy way to reach your entire network—current customers, past customers, and referral sources—all at once, with the click of a button.

Every single business should be sending out a monthly email newsletter—and depending on the size of your business and the size of your customers list, you should strongly consider a print newsletter too.

What goes into your newsletter?

The first thing to understand is that 99 percent of the value is received when the recipient sees it—because that flash of recognition is enough to remind them that you exist and that you're still in business.

Second, to be most effective, your newsletter needs to provide real value to your readers—there needs to be a compelling reason for them to pay attention. So the old, boring, narcissistic style of newsletter—recapping new hires and staff birthdays—isn't going to fly.

Instead your newsletter needs to deliver content that is relevant and useful to your readers. What a crazy idea!

Think back to the exercise we did earlier in this chapter. What are some of the needs, questions, problems, and concerns that your past customers are likely to experience?

Create content speaking to those issues. Write an article or shoot a video. Then put that content into your newsletter each month.

The idea is to create content that is relevant and useful to your readers while at the same time reminding them of the type of work that your business does and the great results that your business provides for your customers. This keeps you top of mind and keeps them primed to send referrals.

You can also create content that's fun for the sake of being fun—cartoons, comic strips, or a joke of the month.

As you're creating this content, it's important to inject some personality into it!

Your newsletter can quickly become dull and boring, so look for opportunities to share your personality, your sense of humor, your unique perspective on the world—the more you can communicate your authentic self, the more your newsletter is going to resonate with your audience.

Include a call to action in your newsletter. A link to schedule an appointment, for example. Your goal is to make it quick and easy for a reader to schedule an appointment—or forward the newsletter to a friend so *they* can schedule a consultation.

By the way—if you'd like a simple template that you can follow to create your own monthly newsletter, we've got one available. Just scan the QR code or visit www.AutomaticMarketingMachine.com/Newsletter to download the template.

One of the questions we hear all the time at our workshops is this: *"Who should I send my newsletter to? Do I send it to my entire contact list?"*

And our answer is: anyone you know who could possibly be in position to (a) buy your products and services, (b) refer someone to your business, or (c) know someone who may be in a position to do business with you or refer someone to your business.

Which means just about everyone on your contact list should receive your newsletter!

"But what if they don't want to receive my newsletter?"

Then they'll unsubscribe!

And unless they are a total jerk, they won't think twice about the fact that you sent them an email newsletter. Meanwhile, the other 99 percent of your contacts that *are* happy to receive your newsletter will be receiving regular content that keeps them engaged and primed to send you referrals.

We share this because many, many entrepreneurs are very concerned about irritating their contacts by sending them an email newsletter.

And while, admittedly, a very small percentage of the population will be irritated to receive an email, the vast majority of your contacts will look forward to it or at least be neutral on the subject. So don't hold back when building your distribution list, as long as you're sure to add people that you legitimately know and have a relationship with. (We don't want you out there spamming people.)

And remember—your newsletter *must* provide value to your readers. It must provide them with educational, informational, or entertaining content in some capacity. If you're not providing value, your audience won't be very engaged.

One final note: Both of us have used email and print newsletters for many years. Despite the fact that there's nothing flashy or exciting about a newsletter strategy, our newsletter campaigns have produced an extremely high ROI over the years.

Print newsletters in particular are very interesting—because people tend to store them on their desk, or in their backpacks, or in their briefcase for a *long* time ... and very often you hear "I've been carrying this thing around for months, and I finally pulled it out, and that's why I finally called to set an appointment."

Also keep in mind that print newsletters are more expensive—which is why you start your print campaign with a small, curated list of your best customers and prospects.

Make sure to download our simple newsletter template that you can customize and deploy in your business:

Visit www.AutomaticMarketingMachine.com/Newsletter to get your template.

LIFETIME VALUE MAXIMIZING SYSTEM #3: SOCIAL MEDIA EARN-BACK CAMPAIGNS SPECIFICALLY TARGETING PAST CUSTOMERS

A third big opportunity to maximize your customer lifetime value is through social media marketing. Social media provides a scalable, low-cost platform to create repeated touchpoints with your customers, past customers, and referral sources.

Repeat: It's *not* just for attracting *new* customers and clients—in fact, one of the very best ways you can use social media is for the specific purpose of keeping your network of customers, past customers, and referral sources engaged.

Let's cover the basics:

Every business—at minimum—should have a Facebook business page. Keep in mind that a business page is *different* from your personal profile. Your personal profile is used to connect with friends, share pictures from your latest vacation, etc. Your business page, on the other hand, represents your business and can be used to run a wide variety of campaigns, including paid advertisements. If this all sounds like gobbledygook to you, enlist the services of a social media–savvy team member to determine whether you have a Facebook business page in place or whether you need to create one.

Most business owners should *also* have a LinkedIn profile. LinkedIn is most effective for business-to-business marketing, but even if your business is consumer facing, you probably have a lot of potential referral sources on LinkedIn—which means you should have a presence there as well.

It's not enough just to have a presence—you need to post content regularly in order to stay engaged with your network. It doesn't have to be you, personally, doing this. But *somebody* on your team should be—whether it's an employee or an outside vendor.

> ## It's not enough just to have a presence—you need to post content regularly.

So what type of content should you post?

Very similar to your newsletter, your content needs to be valuable and relevant to your audience in order to keep them engaged. Tips, strategies, how-to articles, breaking news that matters to your customers, content that's fun just for the sake of being fun, etc.

Keep in mind that <u>video</u> content far outperforms everything else on social media. If you're not using video on social media, you're missing out.

Now here's another secret weapon:

You can actually use social media ads to specifically target your past customers and clients.

We won't get too technical—but essentially, you can upload your email list to social media platforms like Facebook, Instagram, and LinkedIn, and those platforms will then match the email addresses with individual users to create what's known as a list-based audience.

You then have the ability to run earn-back campaigns delivering targeted messaging specifically to your past customers. This strategy alone is worth millions of dollars to your business if you act on it!

Scan the QR code below or visit www.AutomaticMarketing Machine.com/EarnBack for a step-by-step lesson on how to build this type of campaign.

LIFETIME VALUE MAXIMIZING SYSTEM #4: OLD-FASHIONED DIRECT SNAIL MAIL

We get it! It's not fancy! It doesn't have the whiz-bang factor everyone loves to get excited about.

Digital marketing vendors probably tell you it's too old school.

But here's the cool thing about direct mail, especially today: it's precisely because it's fallen out of favor that it works especially well!

Years ago, you might remember that it was totally normal to get a huge pile of junk mail in your mailbox each day.

If you've been paying attention, you have probably noticed that you're receiving less and less every month as compared to even a few short years ago.

Which means *your* old-school direct mail has a better chance to stand out because you're competing against a dwindling set of advertisers.

Even better, with a little creativity—and not a lot of money—you can take steps that will *really* cause your mail to stand out from the pile by adding dimension to it, so that when the recipient opens their mail and they're leafing through it and sorting it into piles, your mail will stand out from the rest.

It can stand out because it makes a noise, or because of its shape, or because of something printed outside of the package, or it can even stand out because of what you've used as a package delivery service.

We've had customers get a tremendous ROI by mailing out a take-out food container as the envelope! We had another use old-school bank bags as the package.

Did you know that the post office will even mail a coconut?

Now, obviously, you're going to have to be thoughtful and strategic about how you build your list. These campaigns are going to be more expensive to deliver than your typical digital campaign, for example. So you have to be strategic … but if you have the right customer list and a solid strategy to maximize lifetime value, investing in an old-fashioned direct mail campaign can be *extremely* profitable.

Stop Flushing Dollar Bills Down the Drain

The vast majority of businesses across the country don't give any thought to maximizing the value of their customer relationships. And they're missing, frankly, very easy opportunities to grow their revenue by 50 percent or more.

So, given that you're already doing the <u>relatively hard</u> work of building your front-end marketing, please don't fail to do the <u>relatively easy</u> work of maximizing the back-end value.

Your Automatic Marketing Machine can't run at maximum power until you've got systems in place to maximize customers' lifetime value.

CHAPTER THIRTEEN

MANAGING YOUR MARKETING TEAM

B y now you've got a burning question.

In the first twelve chapters of this book, we've laid out a simple blueprint for building a simple but reliable Automatic Marketing Machine that will produce a steady supply of new prospects for your business.

But the obvious question you're probably asking is … *"How do I get this all done? How do I execute and actually build the machine? Do I really have to do all this work myself?"*

The answer is no, you do not, should not, and almost certainly could not do all this work on your own. Especially when you're busy running your business!

You *do* have an important role to play, however.

You are the primary driver of the vision of your business, and you'll always want to keep a close eye on your Automatic Marketing Machine to be sure that it's performing to your expectations.

In other words, you'll want to monitor the metrics to be sure none of your vendors or team members are undercutting your highly profitable Automatic Marketing Machine. Either way, you're going to want to use the KPIs we've provided at www.AutomaticMarketingMachine. com/KPI to be sure no one has screwed things up for you.

And here's a word to the wise … it would be a very good idea to periodically spot-check your marketing machine by visiting your own website or websites, opting into your various marketing campaigns, and watching to be sure the follow-up and everything else is happening the way that it's supposed to.

So no, you don't have to build all the components of your marketing machine yourself.

We've asked you to build out your call-me-now campaign and a very simple nurture campaign in earlier chapters only so you can understand the fundamentals and see it all working for yourself … so that you don't buy into the stories of the bucket sellers who would have you lugging water back and forth from the river to keep your business alive, using their leaky buckets!

What you should do is find the right external marketing vendors and, depending on the size of your business, eventually bring some of those roles in house with your own marketing team.

So you might now be wondering … how do we find these people? After all, we just wrote half a book about how half the marketing vendors out there don't understand this stuff and the other half, who do, don't want *you* to understand it!

Good news: That's what the rest of this chapter is about.

How to Leverage External Vendors to Build Your Automatic Marketing Machine

You'll probably want to use external marketing service providers to build and manage many of the more technical components of your marketing machine. Tasks like the following:

- creating your lead magnets—preferably by interviewing you and/or leveraging content you already have

- building and managing your landing pages

- managing your lead-gen ads (which drive traffic to your landing pages)

- creating and managing your follow-up sequences

- producing video content—preferably by directing you in front of the camera

- building and managing your website

You'll need to leverage outside vendors for these tasks because they're highly technical, specialized processes that require a great deal of time and attention. Most small businesses don't have anyone on their team who can build and manage these types of processes cost effectively, and so it makes sense to leverage an outside expert.

However—and we can't possibly state this strongly enough—**you *must* carefully vet and manage your external marketing providers.**

Collectively, over the last twenty-five years or so, we have worked with *many dozens of different* marketing vendors and agencies. And if you count freelancers, that number grows into the hundreds. And if you count all the vendors, in-house staff, and agencies employed by the thousands of small businesses that RJon's company manages, the number of marketing vendors and agencies climbs into the thousands.

We probably should have said this in the beginning of this book, but as they say, truth is stranger than fiction, and in this case the truth is so outrageous that it borders on the implausible. But the math is the math, and implausible as it may seem to be, we have either worked directly with or indirectly cleaned up the mess left behind by *thousands* of marketing vendors, agencies, and freelancers.

Hopefully this helps you understand why we feel as strongly as we do about the topics we've been talking about in this book.

Because your business is supposed to serve your life, and it's supposed to generate revenue by helping your customers or clients or patients have a better life.

And none of that can happen when your marketing vendor or your marketing agency has you hauling buckets instead of helping you build an Automatic Marketing Machine.

Sadly, the list of marketing service providers that have impressed us with their skill, their integrity, and—most of all—their ability to produce results is *very short*.

The vast majority of marketing agencies and service providers out there simply do not serve their clients at a high level. And so most business owners are paying a lot of money for marketing that *does not work*.

Now, it's easy to blame marketing agencies—and they do deserve their fair share of blame. But a lot of the frustration and general lack of results has to do with the fact that *most business owners have no idea how to manage their marketing vendors.* And so, left to operate without structure and without accountability, most marketing vendors predictably fail.

So here are four rules to help you manage your marketing vendors effectively:

RULE #1: DON'T LET YOUR VENDORS DICTATE YOUR MARKETING STRATEGY

You're hiring vendors to build your marketing machine in accordance with the blueprint that you have designed, based on the principles in this book. You *should not* hire marketing vendors and give them free rein to modify your blueprint.

If you were to hire a builder to build a home for you, you'd expect them to follow the blueprint that you and your architect created. Your job is to decide with your architect what you want your home to look like … where you want the bedrooms, where the playroom is located, what the kitchen looks like.

And then you would hand those plans to the builder. The builder doesn't get to then decide, "Hey, wait a minute, I think this house doesn't need a playroom, and I'm going to make the kitchen smaller, and I'm going to put the bathroom here instead."

This might sound funny, but seriously, if you give your marketing vendors the freedom to modify your strategic blueprint … nine times out of ten, they will quickly redesign your machine in a way that makes their life easier and helps them avoid accountability.

That's not to say that you can't include them in strategic conversations—you can and should because they need to understand the big picture. But do not allow them to modify your strategic blueprint without an extremely compelling, data-driven, results-oriented reason to do so.

Remember that fundamentally, **your goal is different from their goal.**

Your goal is to create an Automatic Marketing Machine that generates a steady flow of qualified prospects to your business. Their goal is to keep collecting retainer payments. Never forget this.

RULE #2: DEVELOP CLEARLY DEFINED, OBJECTIVE, MEASURABLE PERFORMANCE INDICATORS BEFORE YOU ENGAGE A VENDOR.

You need to have KPIs in place before you spend a dollar on a marketing campaign. And you need to decide on those KPIs before you hire your marketing vendor.

As an example, imagine you're a CPA and you're about to hire a marketing vendor to build out a lead-generation funnel for your firm. You're asking them to create a lead magnet, build a landing page, and then run ads that drive traffic to your landing page.

Measurable performance indicators for this type of campaign would include

- cost per impression created by the ad campaign,

- cost per click driven by the ad campaign,

- conversion rate of the landing page,

- number of appointments scheduled through your nurture sequence,

- and finally, the total cost per qualified lead generated by the campaign.

Before engaging your vendor, discuss these performance indicators and your expectations. Ask them to commit to measuring and reporting on this data prior to beginning the engagement.

If you'd like help developing these performance indicators, make sure you scan the QR code to download our marketing KPI template or visit www.AutomaticMarketingMachine.com/KPIs.

Have these conversations up front, before you engage your vendor. And then review the KPIs you've agreed on at a regular cadence—quarterly, at least, and probably on a monthly basis until you get your campaigns performing well. This discipline will save you an enormous amount of time, money, and frustration.

RULE #3: CAREFULLY VET YOUR VENDORS BEFORE YOU HIRE THEM

Most small business owners hire a marketing agency based on the recommendation of a friend or colleague.

The problem is that most other business owners have no real criteria when choosing or managing their marketing vendor. So they wind up making referrals based on whether they like their main point of contact at their agency or not. Well, we have had to fire plenty of marketing agencies and vendors whom we liked a lot, personally. We're not hiring friends.

Most business owners have no real criteria when choosing their marketing vendor.

We had to fire them because of the one question that really matters: Does it work? And the answer was objectively no. So they had to go.

So before you act on a friend's or colleague's recommendation of a marketing agency—no matter how much your friend may personally like them—ask the following questions:

- Does the vendor provide you data to show whether your campaigns are working?

- Has the vendor helped you do the strategic work of mapping out your market, message, media fit?

- Did the vendor bother to find out what *your* ideal prospects look like?

- Does your vendor provide you with mission-critical metrics like the cost per lead of each campaign? And the cost of acquisition?

- Are the leads your vendor is providing for you actually qualified? Or is he selling you buckets full of muddy water?

If your friend or colleague doesn't have good answers, don't take their referral too seriously—because obviously, their vendor is just selling them buckets! (What you should do is hand your friend or colleague a copy of this book so that they can learn how to manage their marketing vendors and stop lugging buckets all day, every day!)

But if they give you the right answers, then take the following questions into your conversation with the vendor that's been recommended to you:

- Is the vendor familiar with the principles of direct response marketing, as discussed in this book? Review the ten foundational rules presented in chapter 5 together and confirm that the vendor is willing to follow them.

- Does the vendor have experience working with other small businesses similar to yours, and has the vendor achieved measurable, objective results for them?

- Is the vendor willing to provide you with a reference check so that you can speak to other clients and hear what it's *really* like to work with them? (And then when you do speak to them, ask them the questions that we shared earlier in this chapter!)

- Does the vendor have specific expertise with the type of campaign you need them to create? An agency might be great at SEO, for example, but if you're hiring them to build a lead-gen funnel, their SEO expertise isn't going to help. Make sure that they're capable and experienced in doing the specific type of work you're engaging them to do.

PS—if you have a marketing vendor that meets this criteria, by all means please submit their information using the contact form on our website! We're constantly looking for quality marketing vendors to refer work to. We'd love to meet them.

RULE #4: IF YOU'RE NOT SEEING RESULTS, PULL THE PLUG

If you've followed rule number two and agreed on objective KPIs to measure the success of your campaigns, if you've developed the discipline to meet with your marketing vendors to review your KPIs on a monthly basis (at least), it will actually be refreshingly *easy* to know whether you're on course or not.

If your campaigns are *not* meeting expectations after a reasonable amount of time, meet with your vendor and come up with an action plan to improve performance. If your adjustments don't work ... pull the plug. That doesn't necessarily mean you have to stop working with the vendor—if you like them and trust them—but it means you need to change tactics and take a new approach.

Remember—even the most successful marketers in the world can't guarantee the success or failure of any particular campaign. Marketing is an inexact science because you're dealing with people (your prospects) who aren't always predictable and certainly aren't always rational. So don't get discouraged if one campaign fails.

Where most business owners go wrong is that they don't <u>detect</u> failed campaigns. Because they don't have KPIs in place and because they're not monitoring performance, they have <u>no idea</u> whether a given campaign is working or not. And so for *years* they'll continue shoveling cash down a black hole simply because they don't know how to measure performance.

The problem isn't failed campaigns. The problem is not knowing when your campaigns are failing.

And you can't rely on your marketing vendors to tell you that. You have to demand the data.

Remember, for a list of vetted, certified marketing vendors, visit www.AutomaticMarketingMachine.com/vendors.

ALL MARKETING AGENCIES ARE NOT CREATED EQUAL—NOR DO THEY DO THE SAME THINGS

The term *marketing agency* is so overused that it's almost meaningless. What exactly *is* a marketing agency? It could be a five-hundred-person firm that provides media production services for billion-dollar international companies. Or it could be a guy sitting at Starbucks on his laptop. Neither is necessarily better than the other!

Some marketing agencies specialize in specific verticals, like legal or financial or medical. Others are generalists.

Some marketing agencies specialize in specific services, like SEO or paid search. Others offer every service under the sun. Most of the time, you're much better off working with an agency that focuses specifically on the services you're looking for. It's very rare to find a one-stop shop that executes a huge menu of different services at a high level.

How to Leverage Your Internal Team to Build Your Automatic Marketing Machine

Your external marketing vendors should do most of the heavy lifting. But your internal team should play a supporting role as you build your marketing machine.

Ideally, as your business grows, you'll have an internal marketing coordinator or marketing manager who can keep all your marketing efforts on track. This person is going to handle the mountain of boring, tedious, frustrating, but very necessary work of finding, managing, and communicating with your vendors.

Your marketing coordinator will do things like

- **finding and managing marketing vendors** (using the resources and information we just provided in the previous section!)

- **handling day-to-day communications with your marketing vendors** (because there will be an endless stream of requests, questions, roadblocks, etc., and you do *not* want to deal with all of them yourself)

- **managing "simple" marketing tasks in house** (for example, managing your monthly email newsletter can often be done more efficiently by your internal team; your marketing coordinator may also be able to handle your organic social media accounts)

- **creating and curating marketing content** (it's hard for an external vendor to create your marketing content since they're not present in your business on a daily basis; your marketing coordinator can snap photos, shoot video, and come up with spur-of-the-moment campaigns for social media)

To really build out and manage your Automatic Marketing Machine, you will need internal marketing help. There is a tremendous amount of communication and project management required as you build out your Automatic Marketing Machine, and you simply won't be able to keep up with all of it on your own—unless you're willing to sacrifice everything else in your business!

As a result, you'll drop the ball—and your marketing vendors will take your lack of engagement as a license to do whatever they feel like doing rather than sticking to your plan. You've got to have help.

(By the way, do you need some help finding someone for this role? We've got a marketing coordinator job description available on our website—you can download it and customize it for your business.

Scan the QR code or visit www.AutomaticMarketingMachine.com/coordinator to download your copy instantly.)

But you will always have a role to play as the owner of your business. The buck stops with you. The vision and the strategy will be driven by you. And you have to create a culture of accountability—if you don't demand accountability, your staff and your vendors certainly aren't going to provide it to you.

At minimum you need to be reviewing marketing performance reports on a quarterly basis to ensure that your Automatic Marketing Machine is operating properly—and to demand corrections if it's not.

It Takes a Team to Bring Your Marketing Machine to Life

This book—and the multitude of supporting resources provided on our website—will give you the vision and the blueprint to develop your Automatic Marketing Machine. But as you've certainly realized by now, you cannot build and manage it by yourself—nor should you try.

Your internal staff has a valuable supporting role to play. And your external marketing vendors will perform the heavy lifting. Use the tools and resources provided in this chapter to vet them, manage them, and hold them accountable.

CHAPTER FOURTEEN

THE TALE OF TWO ENTREPRENEURS

T o borrow from Charles Dickens, we're going to wrap up here with the Tale of Two Entrepreneurs.

The story of these two entrepreneurs is really important because it makes clear the sharp contrast between how most business owners attempt to market their business and how a business owner who understands and embraces the concepts presented in this book markets their business.

So, with that said, here is ...

The Tale of Two Entrepreneurs

Consider this tale of two small business owners we know. These are based on two very real people. But for obvious reasons, we've anonymized the details to protect the guilty.

Both are in their early forties; both are happily married with great kids about the same ages. Both operate in the same industry and in similar-sized markets. And even though this story revolves around one particular industry that they both practice in, we trust that by now you know enough to recognize that industry doesn't matter in the least, as this same story plays itself out by the thousands all over the country in every industry you can think of.

We'll call them Andy and Betty.

Andy and Betty are both attorneys who graduated from good law schools with good grades. They both got good jobs at good law firms, where they had good mentors who taught them how to be very good lawyers.

Around the same time, five years ago, for totally different reasons, Andy and Betty each decided to start their own law firm.

Andy thought he could make more money on his own and have a bigger positive impact on the world practicing law his way. So he rented space in a small office in his hometown and got down to business.

Betty hit the glass ceiling one too many times and was left out of too many important meetings that took place at the urinal; plus, she found herself unofficially on the "mommy track" after giving birth to her second child. Finally fed up, Betty left to start her firm in the same town as Andy did at around the same time.

ANDY'S STORY

Andy believes that all it will take to be successful is, first and foremost, to be a great lawyer and do the same kinds of marketing his peers do, and plenty of clients and cases will show up on his doorstep.

He doesn't want to limit in any way the types of clients and cases he takes, which is made abundantly clear by the slogan on his business card, which might as well say "I'll Do Legal Work for Anyone Who

Can Pay Me." And because he figures the majority of his business will come from referrals, he has printed a little note on the back that says "Referrals Welcome!" He thinks that's pretty clever.

Andy puts up a website (with the help of an agency that promises to put him on the first page of Google) loaded with every keyword phrase associated with *legal* possible—*divorce attorney, estate planning attorney, wills and trusts, accident victim, workers' rights, criminal defense,* and so on. The site makes it clear that Andy's little law firm is willing to handle everyone and everything—in fact he went out of his way to be sure there was nothing on the website that could possibly dissuade anyone with any kind of legal problem from picking up the phone and calling for an appointment, and the sooner the better! The site focuses on Andy the Lawyer and the schools he went to and even has a professionally done photo of him at his office in front of a bookshelf crammed with legal books.

Andy runs an ad in the local newspaper that looks exactly like the ads most of his peers use … he doesn't want to stick out, like some kind of weirdo. It lists his phone number and offers a free consultation, just like everyone else does.

He does manage to get clients, and he does provide them with excellent service, but once their case is finished, there's never any kind of continued outreach. After all, Andy did a great job; he's sure they'll remember him when it comes time for any other legal services they may need. And besides, Andy doesn't want to be pushy.

Andy does all the things he was told by all the other lawyers at his local bar association that they're doing to bring in business—being a great lawyer, putting ads in the paper, sponsoring a Little League team, going to local networking events, and so on.

But after five years, Andy's law firm is still just him and an assistant working out of three rooms. He hasn't taken a vacation in years. And lately, Andy notices that he's begun making fewer long-term strategic decisions about where he wants his business and his life to be … and more tactical decisions about how to make payroll and rent at the end of the month. Of course, Andy doesn't turn down any business, and so after five years he's handled about 100 divorces, 150 criminal matters, and a few dozen bankruptcies. Andy also writes wills once in a while and handles the occasional real estate closing. Andy is broke, worried all the time about where the next case will come from, and professionally unfulfilled. But he is very popular among his peers because Andy is a good guy and a good lawyer.

BETTY'S STORY

Betty studied the principles of direct response marketing. She understands that she can't be all things legal to all people, so she decides to narrow her focus to helping the clients with whom she already has a natural affinity—professional women who have experienced workplace discrimination.

She thinks long and hard and creates a message specifically for this demographic: *"I am the lawyer I wish I could have hired when I ran into the glass ceiling—I* guarantee *you'll be treated with the care and respect you deserve."*

Betty creates a lead magnet and headline that also speaks to her *who: "If you're a woman and you've faced illegal job discrimination, call XXX-XXX-XXXX today to get my free report—'Know Your Rights: Seven Strategies to Make Sure Your Employer Treats You Fairly … and What You Can Do about It If None of These Seven Strategies Works for You!'"*

Betty does many of the same things Andy does—she buys an ad in the local paper, she attends networking events, she sponsors a Little League team, she builds a website.

The key difference is that she makes sure that *every* place she shows up, she promotes her messaging and her lead magnet.

Betty's website has a pop-up offering the lead magnet to any visitor who happens to find her. She, too, includes targeted keywords for her website to help with SEO but doesn't bother to include keywords for legal services that aren't top of mind for her ideal target client. She also builds up

> **The key difference is that *every* place she shows up, she promotes her messaging and her lead magnet.**

SEO by blogging regularly on the topic of workplace discrimination—and only on this topic. Each post includes the keyword phrases she knows her prospects use to search for help—and each post includes a call to action to grab her lead magnet.

There's a long video of Betty on the site—all her friends from law school tell her it's too long and that she looks too unprofessional because Betty tells her own personal story and gets emotional when she does. Betty's video is eight minutes long, and indeed, it's a major turnoff to everyone, except the only type of people Betty really cares about attracting—professional women who have been discriminated against in the workplace—they can't get enough!

Betty not only provides great services to her clients, she makes sure to remain in touch using her printed client newsletter, which goes out every month via US mail. It's interesting, fun, and keeps Betty top of mind whenever former clients or people they know need a lawyer.

After five years Betty has handled more than 250 cases of professional women who have been discriminated against in the workplace. She has checklists and templates, and everyone on her team knows just what to do because these cases represent about 80 percent of what the firm does.

Even the reception area is tailored to the unique needs and sensibilities of professional women who have been discriminated against in the workplace. It doesn't look very professional, but when an unemployed woman with young children needs to see a lawyer, it's not always so easy to find childcare, and Betty's clients love it that they're welcome to bring their kids, who love to play with all the toys and games that Betty's staff maintain in a spare room they call the Kids' Office. Betty's reputation has spread, revenues have steadily grown, enabling her to add team members, and now she's looking for a third associate so the law firm can help even more women and handle even more cases.

WHAT *REALLY* HAPPENED HERE ...

Now that we've told the little tale, it's important you understand what's going on in the life of the main character around whom this story and every other story about the success or struggles of a small business revolves:

The *customer*.

Remember, as you step into the story of their life, that they are the center of their story, not you, not your impressive diplomas or fancy office. The customer is the center of his or her own story, not you. You serve a critical role as their advisor, counselor, guide—there to help them navigate through the challenges and drama taking place. But it's not your story that the customer is interested in. It's their own.

And they need you and need you to market as effectively as possible because your prospective customer has a problem that *you* can help them solve.

And so they begin looking for a solution. Of course the only time they've got to look for a solution is the middle of the night, maybe because the problem they need your help with is eating up all their free time during the day, and in any case they've got kids, a job, a relationship, a life, responsibilities.

So, there they are, awake at three in the morning, and they're scouring the internet looking for a solution. Or it's 12:17 p.m., and they're sitting at their desk in the office during their lunch break. Or it's the weekend, and they're glued to their cell phone while the kids beg for attention.

Hooray—they found your advertisement. They found it online. They found it in the newspaper. They found it in an old-fashioned print telephone directory. Or maybe someone they know, like, and trust gave them your name and website address, and they went to your website.

Except then their kid came into the room crying because a bumblebee bit them on the butt.

Except now one of their coworkers has come to their desk to ask a question about the bumblebee that bit their kid on the butt. Except now they are feeling extremely self-conscious looking at your ad because they're not in a place where they have a lot of privacy, and their supervisor is nearby, potentially looking over their shoulder and wondering, "What's going on with her?"

What happens inevitably is the real world intervenes and throws a wrench into your marketing plans, and you never even knew about it—because none of your marketing gave the prospect any way to raise their hand and identify themselves as someone who needs your help.

So then the next day the prospect remembers that they saw your advertising somewhere the day before. They remember that their friend or other trusted advisor gave them your website and they wrote it down somewhere. They take the initiative on their own to go back and find your ad (without getting distracted by anyone else's). They take the initiative on their own to go back to your website, where again they're given no reason and maybe even no way to let you know they're losing sleep and looking for a solution.

They've not learned anything helpful about their situation from you—no free report, no educational video, no invitation to an informative webinar, no nothing; they're just out there on their own, losing sleep, looking for a solution in their spare time.

That is the story taking place out there a million times over for real people with real lives struggling to solve real problems. And you—using typical advertising and marketing methods that you just sort of fell into because everyone else is doing it—are simply hoping that your prospects can make it through this gauntlet of distraction from friends, family, children, pets, coworkers, bumblebees, customers of their own, and everyone else in the world putting advertising in front of them too.

Whoever ends up getting this customer may end up flattering himself or herself that it happened because of their sterling reputation, their awards, or how great their office location is.

Or they may imagine the customers chose them because of how great their products and services are.

And let's not forget all those other business owners who are sitting around, waiting for referrals who imagine the prospect will find them and choose them in that way too.

Point being, absent a trackable marketing system, whoever gets this customer is going to make up every reason in the book for why they got that customer, most of which will be complimentary to themselves and completely wrong.

Of course, they'll also make up reasons why they don't get the customer, which will also be completely wrong—but still complimentary to themselves: the customer is just stupid, other businesses aren't playing fair in their marketing, he has a better office, she has more money to spend on advertising, etc.

We hope you'll keep the Tale of Two Entrepreneurs, Andy and Betty, always in mind to remember the sharp contrast between how most attorneys attempt to market their business and how an entrepreneur who understands and embraces the principles taught in this book does it. You don't have to be like Andy any longer, because now you know how to build your own Automatic Marketing Machine.

Now you have a decision to make. Are you going to act on the principles you've learned in this book? Are you going to build your Automatic Marketing Machine and change the trajectory of your business—and your life—forever? Or are you going to put this book back on the shelf and go back to lugging buckets?

If you're willing to commit and take action, we'll be here to support you through the journey. Doing this all by yourself probably feels overwhelming.

Visit AutomaticMarketingMachine.com, make sure you've downloaded the many tools and resources we've provided for you, and consider attending one of our virtual or in-person workshops. We'd love to meet you face to face.

CHAPTER FIFTEEN

CASE STUDIES

Jennifer Hargrave, Founder, Hargrave Family Law, Dallas, Texas

Hargrave Family Law helps good people end broken marriages. We have been in operation since October 2017 and provide a full range of family law services, focusing primarily on divorce and specifically on collaborative divorce. Conflict is a normal, and even healthy, part of life. However, as a human race, we are inept at handling conflict. My mission in life is to change the way we think about conflict. And it starts in the family. If we can't figure out how to handle and work through conflict in the most basic of human relationships—the family—what hope do we have to be able to resolve even more complex conflicts as a society?

I live and breathe conflict between spouses, and it is my life's work to find a better way to help families in conflict. Marriages don't fail because of conflict—they fail because of unresolved conflict. Unresolved conflict not only destroys the lives it impacts but also has a lasting legacy for generations.

WHO IS YOUR PRIMARY CLIENT?

The clients my firm works with value the family. The decision to divorce was not an easy one. It's often arrived at only after some pretty heroic attempts to save the marriage. Unfortunately, some marriages cannot be saved—often there are personality disorders, abuse, addiction. When my team helps a family transition through the divorce process without the collateral damage of warfare (which is how most divorces are handled), our clients are able to close a chapter in their lives and begin a new chapter of life, love, and success—not only for them but also for their children.

My firm's marketing is designed to attract prospective new clients who

- value the institution of marriage, and

- are selective in the battles they choose to fight, and

- want to preserve and protect the dignity of their family, including the spouse they are divorcing.

Generally, these are sophisticated people who are successful in life. They often have an advanced degree or have advanced in life through their own ingenuity. They are creative. We represent about an equal number of men and women. Our clients have carried the weight of the success of their family, often disproportionately, compared to the other partner.

And nothing makes me happier than to see our clients thrive after divorce. We offer people the opportunity to have a divorce that is consistent with their values and allows them to honor a significant part of their life that has now come to an end.

DESCRIBE HOW YOU DISCOVERED
DIRECT RESPONSE MARKETING

I thought marketing meant trying to impress somebody with how smart or successful I am—I thought it was about showing off the accolades and letting them see how good our firm is at making sausage. My prior sales conversations were basically a tour of the sausage factory. And my firm's marketing was focused on me. I have discovered the principles of direct response marketing through my involvement with How to Manage a Small Law Firm. They taught me to get into the mind of my client. To think about what they are struggling with right now—to speak to those pain points. Now my marketing is focused on my client and the resources my firm has available to help our clients through one of the most difficult journeys in their life.

DESCRIBE HOW YOU ATTRACT YOUR IDEAL CLIENT

The lead-gen strategy that is currently working best for us offers a video introducing collaborative divorce that invites people who are interested to download the *Collaborative Divorce Guide*, which is followed up with a series of emails inviting them to schedule a consultation with the firm.

WHAT'S YOUR ENGAGEMENT PROCESS?

First, they receive a confirmation email with the details of their appointment and the information we ask them to provide ahead of time ... which is not the same information most family law firms are asking for ahead of time. What we've learned from How to Manage a Small Law Firm is to ask for very different information, and it has literally acted like a magnet by accelerating the prospective new client toward a decision to engage the firm even before they come to their first meeting with us!

Second, they receive an email with a video from me—talking about what to look for when hiring a family lawyer. This helps set their expectations, gives them criteria by which to evaluate us, or any family law firm, and keeps accelerating them—like a magnet—toward wanting to hire our firm and only our firm.

Third, they receive a phone call the morning of that confirms their meeting (and follow-up for any info we haven't yet received).

Prospects will meet with an attorney for a paid-for consultation. The fee is $350, and they pay in advance when the appointment is booked. Before we began building an Automatic Marketing Machine, it was much more of a challenge to get appointments booked; now it's pretty much a nonissue for the right kinds of clients, which is pretty great, too, because it protects my team from having to meet with people who aren't going to resonate with what we do.

Following the consultation—if they don't hire right away—they go into one of three buckets:

Option A: Firm declined representation. Client was not a fit. We send a confirmation email that we are not going to accept their case. We likely will not pursue any future correspondence with this individual.

Option B: Client declined representation—client not interested in firm. We send a follow-up email thanking them for considering us. They will also be added to our newsletter emailing list. And we schedule them for a follow-up call to check with them in a few weeks to see how they're doing, because we really do care.

Option C: Client interested but not ready. We have a series of emails to nurture this relationship and help provide additional resources to them. We will also follow up with phone calls and will add them to our newsletter emailing list. Before I discovered the Automatic Marketing Machine, I would have thought this was too pushy. Now I realize it's really the right thing to do to follow up with a person who is going through a very tough time.

DESCRIBE HOW YOU STAY IN TOUCH

We publish a monthly newsletter that is sent by email to everyone in our list (past clients, current clients, friends, family, referral sources).

HOW HAS BUILDING AN AUTOMATIC MARKETING MACHINE CHANGED YOUR LIFE?

This kind of marketing has transformed the way we think about taking care of our clients—not just me but also my whole team. We are building a relationship with our future clients in a way that feels safe to them. This is so important for a family law firm because if a client doesn't feel safe, they're not going to tell you the whole story, and that's always going to hurt your case. By building the relationship in advance, we get more candor from our clients, which helps us do a better job for them.

It's caused a total shift in how I think about the ways we can begin to build connections with people. *Anonymous intimacy* was a phrase I was recently introduced to—people who are struggling in painful marriages are often embarrassed and ashamed to admit they need help.

Our Automatic Marketing Machine helps us attract them into our fold, and now we have a way to begin taking care of them even before they hire us by sharing practical lessons and empowering messages of support and encouragement. This way, when they do become a client of our firm, it's a smooth and organic transition from prospective new client to fully engaged client to former client who is now in a much better position to refer other like-minded people to our law firm. This is a titanic shift in the way I think about my business.

HOWTOFINDMONEYFORCOLLEGE.COM

own a college financial aid planning firm. Our claim to fame is that we cut the cost of college tuition an average of $19,077 per year, per child. Our goal is to help you get your kid to an elite private school for less than the cost of a state school.

WHO IS YOUR PRIMARY CLIENT?

In this business our bread and butter is affluent suburban parents who have really smart, overachieving kids who want to go to a top private university, but they think they can't afford it, they think it's going to cost too much, they think that they make too much to qualify for financial aid, they think they have to settle for a state school, not realizing that the state school's actually going to end up being more expensive, when we're done, than the Stanfords, MITs, or Yales of the world.

HOW DID YOU DECIDE TO TARGET THAT NICHE?

While technically we can help anybody, you know that if you're trying to be all things to all people, you're really nothing to nobody. We narrowed down on that market in a couple of different ways. We arrived at that because number one, we figured out where we can move the needle the most. Most state schools don't have a whole lot of money. They're not sitting on a multibillion-dollar endowment fund like Harvard or Yale or Stanford might be. What we found is, we had better results, saving money, cutting the cost of college, at top private universities that had more money to give away. There are also more misconceptions about the cost of college at private schools than there are about public schools. Most parents don't realize you can get way cheaper education at a private school. Then we had to look at where we can move the needle the most. And then, who can afford to pay us to do that work? And who is going to really appreciate it?

DESCRIBE HOW YOU ATTRACT YOUR IDEAL CLIENT

We pretty much do as many forms of direct response, trackable media as we can. I would say of the three or four biggest things that move the needle for us, number one is that we've built centers of influence. We now have an email list of about eighteen thousand high school guidance counselors. We drip on them every single week with resources, tips, updates to financial aid, updates to college admissions, and every single week, a number of them reply and go, "Oh my God, thank you so much. This was so helpful." We do training webinars for those guidance counselors twice a month, not pitching anything, just giving them resources and free advice to do their jobs better. Because of that, a lot of them respond positively and will do webinars for their school where we host it. They invite all the parents.

I fill a virtual seminar room with no advertising budget whatsoever. We do our presentation for the parents, which is educational, and then there is a pitch at the end, and we have a very good closing rate there, because again, their high school guidance counselor is telling them to work with us. We have another series, another set of centers of influence, where a lot of other financial advisors will refer their clients to us because they don't do college financial aid planning.

A lot of times we will uncover assets that the financial advisor didn't know about, because the parents have to disclose everything to us for the financial aid forms. We send them back to the financial advisor with a teed-up case for them. They're thrilled with us, and they're happy to send us their clients because we won't step on their toes. We'll do the college planning and send the rest back. Those are our two biggest centers of influences: high school counselors and financial advisors. And then in terms of direct-to-consumer marketing, we do a lot of direct mail, a lot of YouTube ads, and a lot of Facebook ads.

WHAT IS YOUR PREENGAGEMENT PROCESS?

There is a multistep drip sequence delivered via email, social media, text message, and direct mail. And then there is a sixty- to seventy-minute training video they have to watch before they can schedule a conversation with us.

I'm trying to eliminate the first appointment. I'm trying to warm them up, indoctrinate them into our world, teach them who we are, what we do, who we do it for, who we can't help, why we do what we do, and why we're different and to give them a ballpark estimate of what they might be in for financially to work with us. So that the only people who then actually schedule meetings are qualified, interested, and pretty much ready to go.

HOW DO YOU MAXIMIZE THE LIFETIME VALUE OF YOUR CLIENTS?

Not only do we have a new-client welcome box, a welcome thirty-days-to-wow drip sequence, not only will we do a great job doing our job and tell them about it, but we promote what we call our ambassador program, where they can earn referral fees, discounts on services, and scholarships by becoming the ambassador for how to find money for college at their high school. And every one of their friends, any one of their parents' friends, who comes in, they get paid. We have students who end up getting our services for free. And we have students who end up almost working at a part-time job, where we're basically paying them to let us serve them because they're bringing us so much business.

HOW HAS THIS STYLE OF MARKETING CHANGED YOUR LIFE?

We've been in business eight years as this entity. Before that I was at a Fortune 500 financial services firm, building my client base, doing this there. I left in '07, when the subprime bubble burst, to go start this firm separately so that we weren't hamstrung by what compliance said we could or couldn't do. And we didn't start with any of this. We literally built it one step at a time. We started running ads, started running direct mail, and scaled up as we went. We've grown our revenues an average of 1,547 percent year over year over year. I've been ranked as high as one of the top thirty college financial planners in the country, based on the results of the marketing that we've built over time.

WWW.CYBERBRIGADE.NET

I started my IT company in 2009, fresh off getting laid off from my job. I kind of fell into this whole entrepreneurial landscape. I didn't know much about marketing. I knew I was good at what I did, which was IT. I kind of fell into it, and really, I didn't know much about marketing. I didn't know much about sales. I just knew I was a good technician. I kind of figured, as long as I'm good at what I do, I can figure out the sales and marketing thing, which we all know is the hardest part of any business. I spent a long time really struggling to figure it out.

I found a mentor by the name of Robin Robins. She helped me to understand what it was that marketing is, how to put systems in place. And from there I found other mentors as well. And really I spent the next couple of years just really becoming more of a marketer in my business and less of a technician. As the owner of the company, I realized that I was responsible for revenue generation. I really dove into marketing.

I found that I love marketing even more than the actual IT work. Over the last several years, I've studied with Russell Brunson and all sorts of different mentors. But really, we've had a lot of success. Even throughout the pandemic, we were marketing. We were bringing on new clients. As some of my competitors were folding, we had our best year ever last year. I sometimes feel a little bad about it.

WHO ARE YOUR PRIMARY CLIENTS?

We have two different divisions of the company. My main focus is on businesses with ten to fifty employees. That's our sweet spot. We're across a range of different industries. We have medical companies. We have a lot of law firms, but we also have some other different business-to-business-type companies.

My other side of my company, which we just launched this year, is helping high-net-worth individuals and solo entrepreneurs to also put effective cybersecurity into place. What I'm finding from going to a lot of these mastermind groups is you'll have either a solopreneur, or maybe he has one or two partners, and because they're not a traditional company, they're kind of getting overlooked by a lot of these cybersecurity and IT firms because they're hard to protect.

We're actually launching a new company specifically to help those types of people. Because just because they're solopreneurs does not mean that they don't have a lot of critical client data, financial information, all this stuff that needs to be protected. Even though they don't have a traditional office with a traditional firewall and all that—they work from coffeehouses and stuff—we're looking to protect them as well.

DESCRIBE HOW YOU ATTRACT YOUR IDEAL CLIENT

We have two different lead magnets that really, really work well for us. One talks about the different ways that companies and individuals get hacked. The other one we have is our IT cost report, which basically tells entrepreneurs what they should expect to pay for IT, because a lot of these guys don't know what they're supposed to pay. They don't know what makes a good IT company from a contract standpoint. They really don't know how to get started. Both of those reports do very well for us.

Basically, once people opt in to that, we have a lead-nurture campaign that directs to a page where they could book an appointment with our sales team right on our Acuity calendar. And from there, they get into our sales process.

WHAT'S YOUR PREENGAGEMENT PROCESS?

As soon as they opt in, they get a welcome sequence. And over the next five days, they get a welcome sequence that talks about us and talks a little bit about my background, a little bit about the company.

But more importantly, we just start to educate them right from day one on the different things they should be looking for, the different threats that they probably don't even know about.

Everything pushes back toward that initial consultation that books on our Acuity calendar and then goes from there. If we see that they're constantly opening our emails, we'll actually pick up the phone and call them up, but most people just book right through the Acuity calendar.

HOW DO YOU MAXIMIZE THE LIFETIME VALUE OF YOUR CLIENTS?

When someone becomes a client, we have an automation that in thirty days creates a task right on my dashboard to follow up with them. I find that following up in person or on the phone gets me a better referral than any sort of automated email does. We bring on only, like, two to three clients a month, so it's not very difficult. But usually I'll reach out, check how they're doing, making sure everything's good.

At that point, I'll say, "Hey, most of the work we do is actually by word of mouth. Is there anyone else you know that could benefit from our services?" Another thing I do is when I have my quarterly meetings with each client, I'll refer back to that, see if they have any other referrals. We get a good number of referrals from our clients.

HOW HAS DIRECT RESPONSE-STYLE MARKETING CHANGED YOUR LIFE?

Oh, it's been amazing. Before I discovered this style of marketing, I was wasting money on Yellow Pages ads and advertising in trade newspapers and all this stuff that never got me any sort of real return that I can measure. But year over year, we've continued to grow at least 25 percent every year for the last nine years. It's been amazing for us.

I work from home. I don't even have a traditional office anymore. Just with the pandemic and everything, we realized that our office was a big expense. But I work from home. I make it to all my kids' activities. I typically work twenty to thirty hours a week because I'm not out there hustling and chasing all these bad leads anymore. My primary driver in my company is driving revenue. And as long as all my systems are working, it gives me a lot more time to enjoy my life, actually.

WHAT'S THE BIGGEST LESSON YOU'VE LEARNED AS YOU'VE BUILT YOUR MARKETING MACHINE?

Number one, no matter what you're doing, make sure it's trackable and measurable. Stop throwing marketing dollars at everything and just seeing what sticks. You really have to focus on a strategy and just measure it. What you want is to put a dollar in, get at least two dollars out, and you know it's a winner, and then you can ramp up. That was the biggest concept for me, understanding my numbers. Understanding, okay, we spent $2,000 on this marketing campaign. We got $4,000 out. So now let's just ramp it up and turn on the fire hose.

Those levers really help every other aspect of my business because then revenue is predictable. I know when to hire. I know when to expand, all that sort of stuff, all by getting my revenue to the point where it's measurable and predictable like that.

For even more success stories and case studies, scan the QR code below or visit www.AutomaticMarketing Machine.com/CaseStudies. You—yes, **you,** no matter what industry you're operating in or where you live or how long you've been in business—can absolutely do this! Let's make it happen.

ABOUT THE AUTHORS

RJon Robins

RJon Robins believes in profit and he detests loss. He's the cofounder and President of How To MANAGE Enterprises and one of its subsidiaries, How To Manage a Small Law Firm (HTM).

After having grown by more than TEN THOUSAND PERCENT since RJon started the business from his dining room table in 2009, How To Manage A Small Law Firm has been named by *Inc.* magazine as one of the 5,000 fastest-growing privately held companies in the country six years in a row. RJon attributes such exponential growth to the success of the thousands of small businesses his own organization helps to manage, and his amazing team whom he is honored to work with.

All of the portfolio companies owned and operated by How To MANAGE Enterprises share RJon's commitment to liberating entrepreneurs from The Doctrine of Sacrifice by helping them build more successful businesses that support happier and more successful and more meaningful lives. RJon practices what he preaches, often working from his boat *The Office* in sunny South Florida when not investing time with his wife and their son.

Danny Decker

Danny Decker spent most of his childhood in West Africa, where his parents were missionaries. Today, he's a serial entrepreneur, marketing strategist, consultant, podcast host, and keynote speaker. Danny started, scaled, and sold his seven-figure marketing agency in just six years—he's passionate about teaching small business owners how to build marketing systems that really work for their businesses.

Danny believes that marketing is the "missing link" that keeps small business owners in every industry from growing their businesses to their full potential. Most business owners didn't study marketing in school–and so, predictably, they fall prey to marketing vendors who take their money but don't deliver measurable results. And their business stagnates. They're not serving as many customers and clients as they could be serving, they're not creating as many jobs as they could be creating, and they're not enjoying the level of freedom and financial success that they could be experiencing. Danny teaches business owners how to cut through the BS and create marketing systems that allow their business to grow to its full potential.

When he's not speaking, writing, or leading a workshop, he enjoys quality time with his wife, their two kids, and their hyperactive German shepherd.

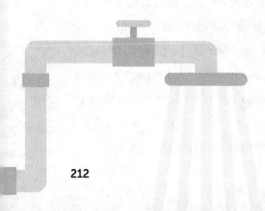

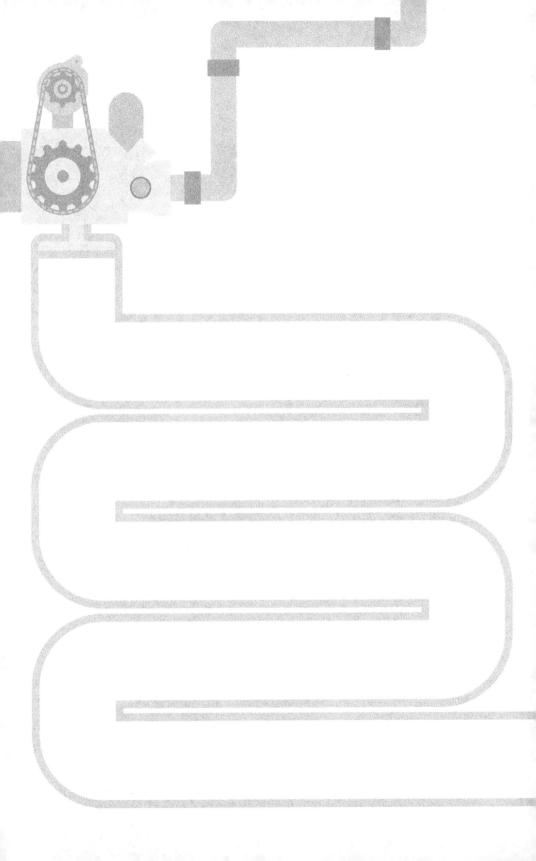

CPSIA information can be obtained
at www.ICGtesting.com
Printed in the USA
BVHW041328250422
635268BV00008B/84/J

9 781955 884143